THE

100%

NATURAL FOODS

COOKBOOK

To Jane Beckwith, for being the best thing
that ever happened to Delta High School,
and nearly single-handedly saving the
history of Topaz Internment Camp, despite
every obstacle erected in your path.

ISBN 13: 978-1-4621-1344-6

Published by Front Table Books, an imprint of Cedar Fort, Inc.
2373 W. 700 S., Springville, UT 84663
Distributed by Cedar Fort, Inc., www.cedarfort.com

Library of Congress Cataloging-in-Publication Data

Warnock, Caleb (Caleb J.), 1973-
The 100 percent natural foods cookbook / Caleb Warnock.
     pages cm
ISBN 978-1-4621-1344-6 (layflat binding : acid-free paper)
1. Cooking (Natural foods) I. Title. II. Title: One hundred percent natural foods cookbook.
TX741.W3685 2015
641.3'02--dc23
                              2015020063

Cover design by M. Shaun McMurdie
Page design by Michelle May
Cover design © 2015 by Lyle Mortimer
Edited by Justin Greer

Printed in China

10 9 8 7 6 5 4 3 2 1

Printed on acid-free paper

THE
100%
NATURAL FOODS
COOKBOOK

CALEB WARNOCK

FRONT TABLE BOOKS

An Imprint of Cedar Fort, Inc. | Springville, Utah

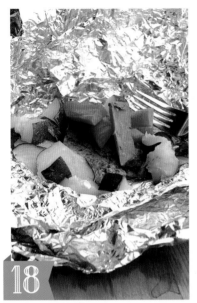

18

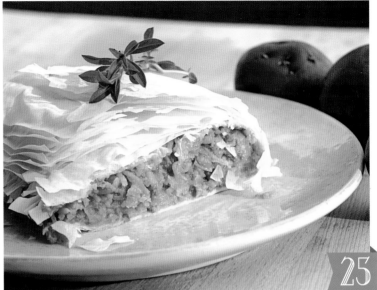

25

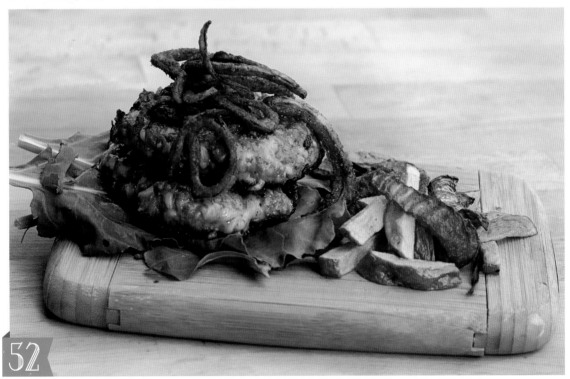

52

Contents

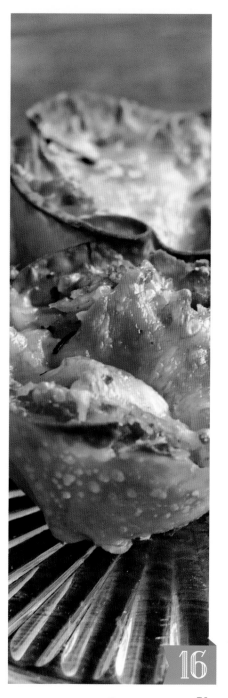

16

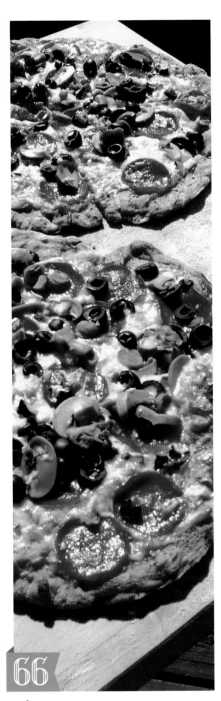

66

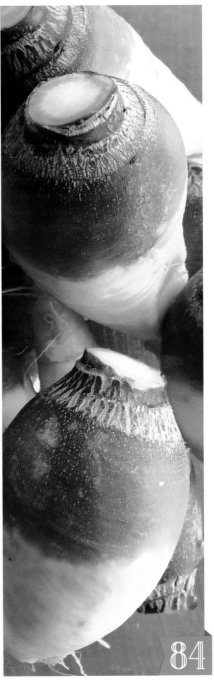

84

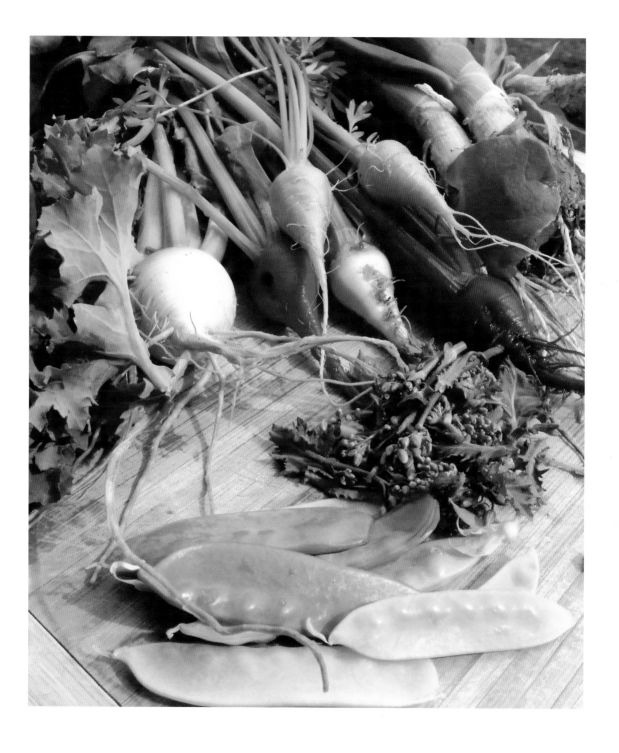

Welcome to the

100% Natural Foods Cookbook

When it comes right down to it, health is often really about food. Families want to eat closer to the earth, to Mother Nature. Our world is awash in fast food and fake food, chemicals and questions about the health effects of what we put into our bodies. We want strength and stamina for ourselves. We want to provide nutrition and a good example for our children and grandchildren. We want food that tastes fantastic, fills us, and gives us comfort and joy. We want the best for the people we love, and the well-being of the earth which sustains us. For these reasons, I have written *The 100 Percent Natural Foods Cookbook*.

In these pages you will find ingredients fresh from the garden or field. Every recipe focuses on using natural foods in ways that are often new and unexpected, relying on forgotten cookery from generations gone by. Whether your vegetables come from your local farmers market, your backyard garden, or your local grocer, this book will help you create quick meals that your family will beg to eat again and again.

After the success of my first four nonfiction books, people began to ask what our family eats. They wanted recipes, photos, and ingredients. They wanted to know how we manage to spend so little money at the grocery store. We relish eating out of our garden–I've often said in books and speeches that I'll put our family's grocery store bill up against anyone's in the nation, and we'll probably win. What do we buy at the grocery store? What don't we buy? Why?

Clearly, you–my readers–are curious to know what everyday natural living really looks like at the table. This book is the answer. But you don't have to grow your own food to join in the good eating. If you don't love to garden, look no further than your local farmers market for growers who are passionate about flavor and freshness at a local level.

As I put this book together, I wrote with you, the reader, in mind. All of us are at different levels when it comes to taking control of, and responsibility for, our health. I've given dozens of speeches over the past year to thousands of people, and I always ask for a raise of hands–how many of you have eaten an all-natural, fresh meal in the past year? Past month? Past week?

I know from your emails, letters, comments on my blog posts, and your questions at my speeches that all of you who love my books want health, a diet of fewer chemicals, and green living. Some of you are just looking for confidence and the right place to start. Some

of you have battled your health and are now looking to eat in a new way. Some of you want to transition from reliance on the grocery store to the freedom of eating from the garden. Some of you are regulars at your local farmers market who simply want more great recipes.

Most people want these things because they want a new standard of health for themselves, their children, and grandchildren. You also want to save money. A return to the example of previous generations will pass to the youth the living gift of a knowledge of true food and real nutrition.

Whether you live in an urban or rural area, and whether you have a balcony, a backyard, or 1,000 acres, there is something lurking in our miserable diet that is wrecking havoc on families. I took on the topic in one of my famously fiery blogs posts at CalebWarnock.blogpost.com:

Hello America. Brace Yourselves to be Cussed Out.

As parents and grandparents, we have a few clear-cut duties. One of them is to know the answer to this question: Am I harming my children with the food I feed them?

The medical condition that is most likely to torture and then kill you and your children as you age is Type 2 Diabetes. This clear and present danger is ignored at your peril.

The way to prevent Type 2 Diabetes is with high-fiber vegetables and naturally prepared grains.

"My husband doesn't like vegetables," you will say as you turn away. "Cooking from scratch might be hard. I'm busy."

Oh! Why didn't you say so earlier?! Run off on your merry way to the prepackaged foods aisle, then, little poppet. You are absolved of personal responsibility, and no natural consequences will hound you.

Okay, that was snarky and I apologize. Sometimes, though, a bit of poking at the soul can get people to sit up and listen.

Aligning ourselves with reality, we have to admit that Americans are not likely to give up sugar, white flour, and soda, which are causing this plague. Even cutting down is difficult–every office in this country is flooded with donuts and treats. There is more shelf space dedicated to candy and soda in your local grocery store than there is space for fresh vegetables–by far. Why? Because the stores give space to what people want to buy.

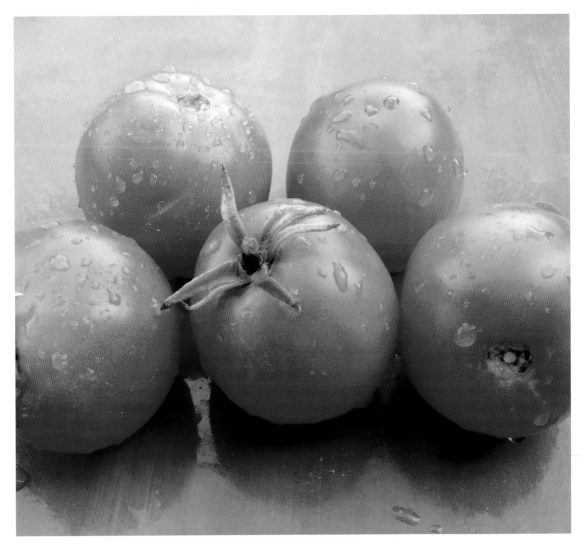

Type 2 Diabetes is why today's children are expected to be the first generation in history with a shorter lifespan than their parents—read that twice.

We are choosing this disease. We are voting with our mouths.

Shockingly few Americans have any knowledge of how to stop the disease that is doing the most harm to our own children. Fiber is the answer.

Starches (white flour, rice, potatoes) are digested by the body exactly like sugar, meaning

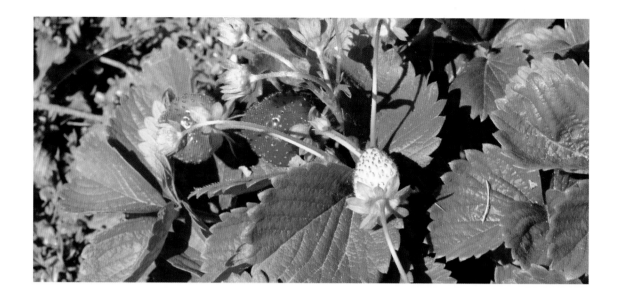

they spike the body's glycemic index exactly like sugar. Over years, spikes in the glycemic index destroy the ability of our pancreas to produce insulin. The body must produce insulin to digest glucose (sugar).

Fiber slows the body's digestion. Fiber is prebiotic, meaning it is the place where the good and necessary probiotic bacteria and fungi in our bodies live. Without both soluble and insoluble fiber, natural probiotics (bacteria and fungi) cannot colonize in our guts. Without fiber, our digestive system struggles and slowly breaks down. Our weakened bodies then fall victim to all manner of autoimmune deficiencies, which are normally staved off by healthy people. (For most people, being genetically predisposed to an autoimmune disorder simply means you will get the disease only if you are not healthy.)

Making matters worse, we use "shock and awe" antibiotics, which kill both what is bad for us and what is good for us--and then we do not replenish our natural probiotics with cultured foods. In addition, when we do bother to put down our sodas to drink a glass of water, our water is chlorinated. Chlorine is put in water to kill flora and fauna. It does the same thing in our bodies. If you have any doubt about this, you can grow natural yeast side-by-side in purified water and tap water and see the difference for yourself.

A healthy gut is a busy metropolis of beneficial probiotic bacteria and fungi thriving on prebiotic soluble and insoluble fiber. Sugars, protein, and carbohydrates are digested slowly, making us feel full while allowing the body to take what it needs. Because we digest slowly, there are no glycemic spikes. Our pancreas functions normally throughout life. We do not get

Type 2 Diabetes. We are happy, healthy, and not morbidly obese. (Caution: 15 percent of people who get Type 2 Diabetes are at a normal healthy weight. This is not just a disease for overweight people.)

Our guts are not healthy. This is proven by the huge surge in Type 2 Diabetes.

Our guts are ghost towns. There are few good bacteria and yeasts, and little fiber for them to call home. Our fake-food diets move through us fast, not slow. This causes us to feel hungry instead of full, which in turn causes us to eat more fake food. We scorch our empty gut with glycemic-spiking sugar and starches, chlorinated water, and antibiotics. Then we develop Type 2 Diabetes, suffer, and die early.

Odds are, this is your future.

This is what awaits our children.

Vegetables can stop all this. Raw, cooked, and cultured vegetables are the answer. Grains prepared with natural yeast are also the answer.

Now that you know the answer, there is just one question left: will you be like most people and decide not to change your vote (by mouth) until you or someone you love has been diagnosed? Or will you change now, so the diagnosis never appears and you and your children live happily ever after?

Vegetables and natural yeast. Or Type 2 Diabetes. Truth is easy. Truth is simple.

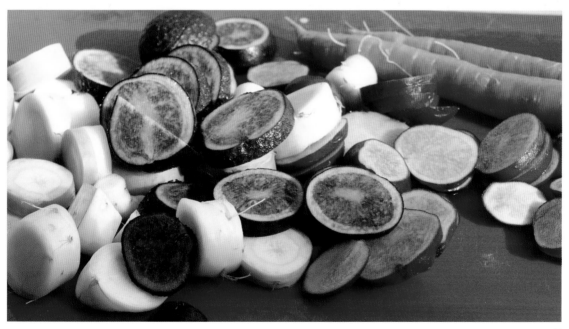

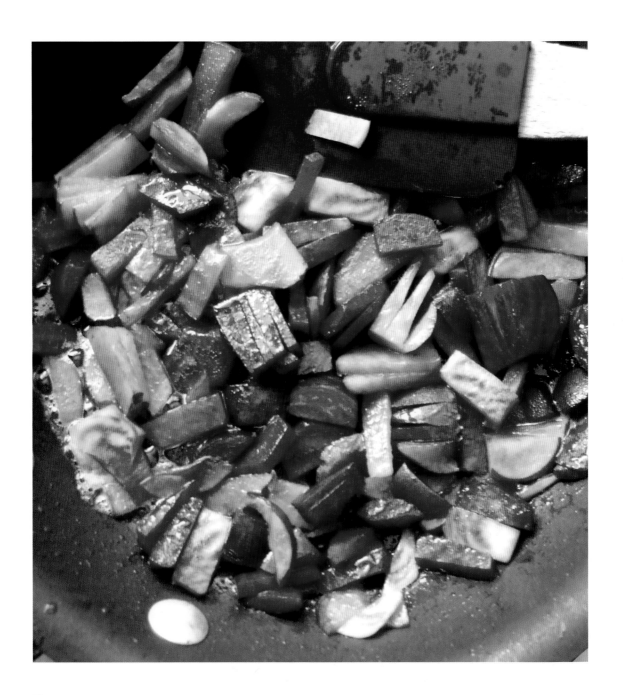

Crudités and Légumes Vapeur

Right at this moment, some of you dear readers are thinking, "What a pretentious writer!" It is a fair accusation. Crudités is the fancy French way of saying fresh raw vegetables eaten as an appetizer, and Légumes Vapeur is the pinky-pointed-out way of saying steamed vegetables. But before you dismiss me as reaching or suffering from delusions of grandeur, let me explain why I think the title of this chapter is important. I have chosen it thoughtfully.

First of all, let's get real. If I had called this chapter "Steamed Vegetables," you would have skipped right past it. "I don't need a book to teach me how to steam vegetables," you would have correctly surmised. Steamed vegetables are booorrrring, and your family is not likely to get too excited if you announce that supper this evening will be steamed roots. But as you will see below, there are ways to prepared both raw and steamed vegetables that are delicious and refreshingly different.

Second, raw and steamed vegetables should be on our dinner table. If you are having steaks or chops, fresh corn with summer or winter savory is a great addition. And there are times–a sweltering summer afternoon or evening, for example–when raw vegetables alone make a great light meal or after-school snack.

Tips

Onions should be part of every steamed vegetable dish because they enhance the flavor of both vegetables and spices.

Raw vegetables can be coated with olive oil for steaming or eating raw. In either case, coat them as lightly as possible. One-third of a teaspoon of olive oil in a bowl is perfect for 1 cup of chopped vegetables.

I peel fresh garden vegetables only as necessary. Vegetables can naturally have divots, small discolorations, and blemishes on their skin. I remove these and everything else stays after a careful scrubbing.

Boiling vegetables and then removing the water also throws out some of the best vitamins. Steaming is considered healthier. Either way, don't overcook the vegetables. Cooked vegetables should be chewy, not mushy. If they fall apart or collapse at the touch of a fork, they are overdone. Here are 21 ways to make your raw, steamed, or sautéed vegetables in new and unexpected ways.

1. **Thyme and Lemon balm (also called Melissa).** Chiffonade fresh leaves of both. Toss the vegetables very lightly in olive oil. Dried herbs may also be used.

2. **Garlic chives.** Mince garlic chives. Toss the vegetables very lightly in olive oil. Dried garlic chives may also be used.

3. **Summer or Winter Savory.** The leafs of these two delicious herbs can be crushed, fresh or dried, and tossed lightly with vegetables and olive oil.

4. **Lemon Beebalm.** The long leaves and purple flowers of this plant can be used to add a strong citrus fragrance and flavor to vegetables.

5. **White pepper and sea salt.** White pepper has a more subtle, less powerful flavor than black pepper, making it a great choice for steamed or raw vegetables. Sea salt really brings out the natural flavor of vegetables. Use only a thin dusting.

6. **Anise.** Anise flowers or seeds have a natural sweetness and licorice flavor. Go light when using this spice. A little goes a long way! Garden anise is a feathery herb and is not the same thing as star anise, which has much larger seed pods and is often used in tea.

7. **Cilantro.** This feathery herb is a favorite among salsa lovers, but it also make a great spice for pasta, salad, and yes, fresh and steamed vegetables. Crush the seeds with a flat mortar and pestle or the flat side of a butcher's knife before sprinkling them on.

8. **Dill.** This herb has a unique and powerful flavor of its own that is especially refreshing in summer heat.

9. **Sweet Basil.** This is the most-used culinary herb in our house. There is not much it doesn't lift to a higher level–soups, stews, roasts, gravy, casseroles, and vegetables.

10. **Lime juice and basil.** I have had a lifelong love affair with lime juice. Sweet pork nachos topped with fresh-squeezed lime juice and romaine lettuce is one of my favorite meals. Yes, I know, not many people eat their nachos with lettuce, but I do! Lime juice pairs perfectly with basil and makes a great glaze for vegetables.

11. **Sesame oil, soy sauce, rice vinegar.** I lived in Japan for two years, and this tasty concoction is perhaps Japan's most popular sauce. The key is to get the ratio correct. Use one part sesame oil to two parts soy and two parts rice vinegar. At our house this is most often served in little individual Japanese sauce dishes (available at Asian food markets).

12. **Pomegranate juice with stevia.** This deep purple healthy juice has a natural tartness that is softened with a bit of stevia extract or thinly chiffonaded stevia leaves. Stevia is a green herb with sweet leaves. I grow stevia in my house, in my greenhouse, and in my garden.

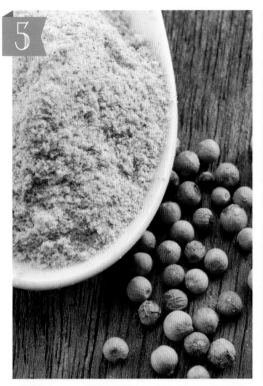

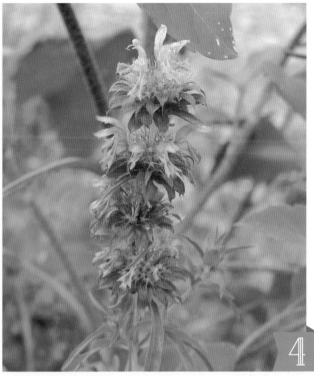

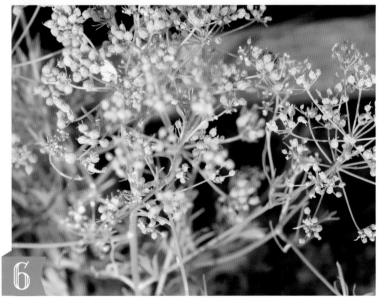

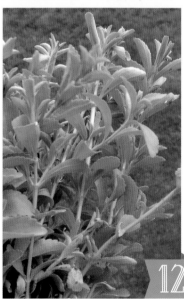

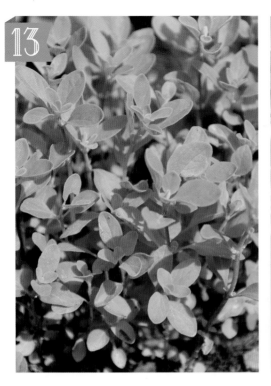

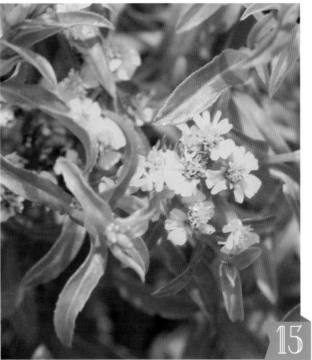

13. Marjoram. This savory herb brings an autumn flavor to vegetables.

14. Clove or cumin. Cumin is a garden herb that can be used as a substitute for clove seeds, which must be ground to powder. Both have a strong flavor that I crave. Clove-dusted carrots glazed in butter are especially mouthwatering. The flavor is earthy, somewhere between cinnamon and the best mushrooms. Caution: a tiny bit of ground clove or cumin goes a long way.

15. Sweet Mace. Most people have never heard of this herb, which produces tiny orange flowers in the garden. It is also called Spanish Tarragon. It has an anise flavor. The leaves and flowers pair nicely with carrots and Albino or Chioggia beets. Seeds for this easy-to-grow herb are available at SeedRenaissance.com.

16. Nutmeg and ginger. This is the flavor of autumn. Powdered nutmeg and ginger is great not only for pumpkin and winter squash, but also for French toast (add it to the beaten eggs before soaking the bread.) These spices are not usually used in combination with onion, unless egg is a prevalent ingredient. For vegetables, nutmeg and ginger pair especially well with winter carrots, Albino beets, and Chioggia beets because of their natural sweetness.

17. Lemongrass. For a light lemon flavor, turn to lemongrass. This plant looks somewhat like garlic chives but tastes like citrus instead. Lemongrass has a lighter, more delicate flavor than lemon balm or lemon beebalm. Seeds at SeedRenaissance.com.

18. Pinenuts. Lightly roasted, these nuts, which grow native where I live, are earthy and nutty. They pair especially well with all vegetables of the brassica family, including Brussels sprouts, cauliflower, broccoli, kale and collards.

19. Balsamic vinegar. True, aged balsamic vinegar has a depth of flavor that works well with most vegetables, especially if you add a tiny dusting of stevia to sweeten the flavor. This dark-colored vinegar, which has been used for more than 1,000 years, is especially good with all vegetables of the brassica family, including Brussels sprouts, cauliflower, broccoli, kale, and collards.

20. Curry powder. One of the best ways that I know to eat cauliflower is to toss it in olive oil, dust it with curry powder, cover, and roast at 350 degrees until tender. This is a flavor pairing you can fall in love with.

21. Garam Masala. This traditional Indian spice blend includes coriander and a hint of cinnamon among a host of other spices. There is nothing else like it in the savory category.

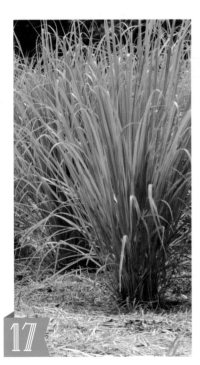

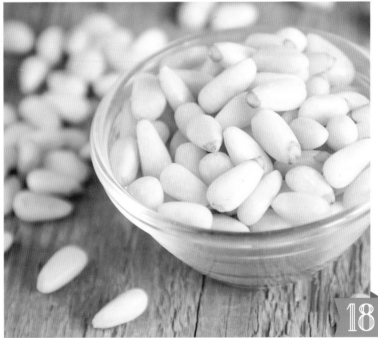

Homemade Vegetable Stock

COOK TIME: OVERNIGHT

For stock, use leftover vegetable pieces and scraps: corn cobs, onion scraps and peels, old but still good vegetables, bits of beans, shells of peas, and peels and skins of roots. Onion, celery or Swiss Chard ribs, and carrots should make up the bulk of your recipe.

Thyme

Parsley

chives

garlic chives

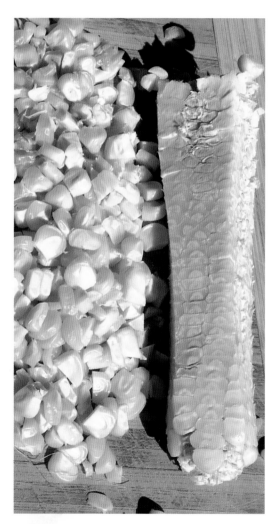

1 Put your vegetables and/or scraps in the crockpot overnight (or for 12 hours) on low. Do not add water. (To avoid a sulpher taste, don't put in much broccoli, cabbage, collard greens, kale, kohlrabi, artichoke, mustard greens, or Brussels sprouts.)

2 In the morning, cool your slow cooker and remove the wilted vegetables from the broth. (You can feed the wilted vegetables to your chickens or compost them.) Strain the broth through cheesecloth. To get every last bit of flavor, put your wilted vegetables in cheesecloth and press out the remaining juices with a spoon. This step is not necessary but does get out some of the best flavored broth.

3 Pour broth into quart jars and store in the fridge or freezer. If you freeze them, leave at least an inch of space at the top of the jar because the broth will expand as it freezes.

Savory Italian Plait

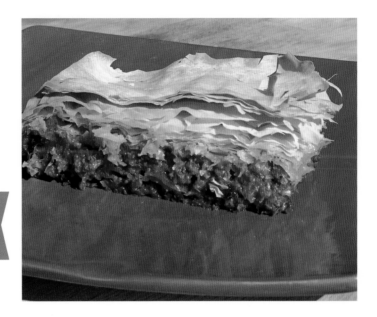

SERVES 6–8
PREPARATION AND COOK
TIME: 45 MINUTES

This is one of my favorite recipes in the world. It makes a wonderful autumn or winter supper, and is based on an old English favorite called Sausage Plait. At our house we "Italianize" it with sweet Italian sausage.

4 large onions

4 large carrots

2 tablespoons olive oil

2 tablespoons butter

1 lb. hamburger

1 lb. sweet Italian sausage

⅓ cup whole wheat flour

1 teaspoon salt

1 teaspoon beef bouillon
  powder

1 quart tomato sauce

1   Dice the onions. Using a peeler, reduce all the carrots to peelings and then chop up the pile of peelings. Heat oil and butter over medium heat in a large, heavy-bottomed pot or enameled cast iron skillet. Add carrots and onions and stir until coated with the oil and butter. Cover the pot and cook on medium heat for 5 minutes.

2   Add in the hamburger and sausage and brown over medium heat. Drain fat if necessary. Sprinkle flour over the mix and stir over medium heat.

3   Add in seasonings and tomato purée. Heat until mixture bubbles. Pour mixture into a 9 x 13 baking dish and cover with one sheet of puff pastry. Bake at 350 degrees for 30 minutes. Serve hot.

Optional: Instead of half sausage and half hamburger, you can use 2 pounds of hamburger. You will need to double the amount of salt and bouillon.

Quick Turkey Supper Pie

MAKES A 1.5-QUART ROUND CASSEROLE DISH
PREPARATION AND COOK TIME: 30 MINUTES

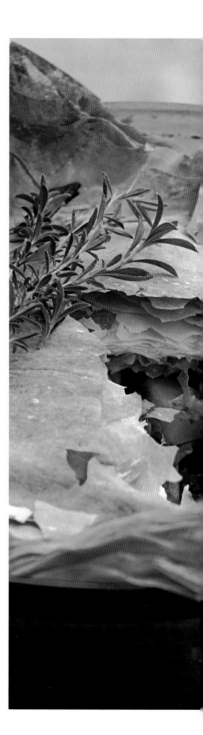

Nothing is as cozy as a turkey supper pie on a cold autumn or winter evening. Only one thing can improve the experience: being able to make the pie in 25 minutes. There are two secret ingredients in this pot pie. The first is oatmeal flour, which gives the gravy the old-fashioned flavor and texture like grandma used to make it. Oatmeal flour is available at health food stores. If you can't find oatmeal flour, you can use regular rolled oats instead. The second is the phyllo dough crust. I love the flakey layers of crunchy filo, but if the papery texture doesn't please you, use puff pastry instead. While turkey is my favorite way to make this dish, you can use any protein. If you choose steak or hamburger, use beef stock.

1 onion

2 tablespoons olive oil

1 tablespoon butter

3 carrots or parsnips, diced

2 beets or turnips, diced

2 potatoes, diced

½ cup Swiss chard ribs or celery, diced

½ cup corn kernels

1 cup cubed cooked turkey

½ teaspoon salt

dash of pepper

¼ teaspoon thyme

¼ teaspoon marjoram

2 cups of stock (turkey, chicken, or vegetable)

2 tablespoons oat flour

½ cup peas

1 roll of prepared filo dough pastry (also called phyllo dough)

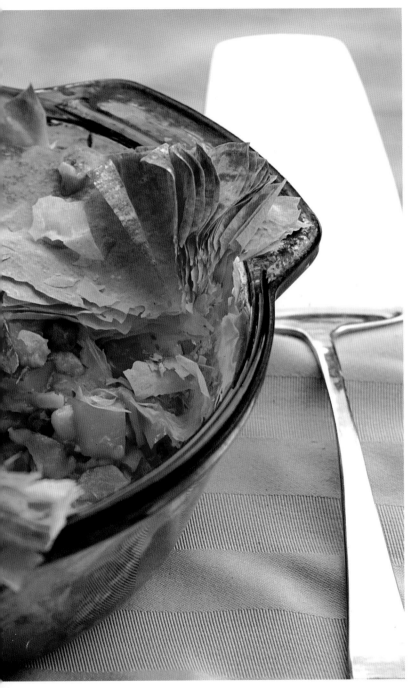

1 Chop the onion. In a heavy pan (enameled cast iron works best) soften the onions over medium heat in the butter and olive oil. This will take about 5 minutes.

2 Add the vegetables (except the peas), meat, herbs, and spices, to the onions and cook another 3 minutes.

3 Pour the stock into the pan and cook until the stock is reduced by half, about 10 minutes.

4 Stir in the oat flour. The mixture will quickly thicken. Turn off the heat. Stir in the peas. Pour the mixture into a round 1.5-quart glass or stoneware baking dish.

5 Cut a square of prepared filo pastry. Cover the casserole dish, allowing the four corners to stick up. Bake at 400 degrees for 10 minutes or until fillo dough is golden brown. Serve warm.

20-Minute Lasagne Tartlets

MAKES 24 TARTLETS OR 48 MINI-TARTLETS
PREPARATION AND COOK TIME: 30 MINUTES

This is a fairly new recipe to our family, but it has become an instant hit because it is so quick to make. If you are cooking for kids, you can substitute parmesan cheese for cheddar and mix the cheddar directly into the meat and vegetable mixture instead of putting it on top. You can remove the meat and double the vegetables if you want a meatless option. To make this recipe in the Indian style, use ½ teaspoon of garam masala spice blend and do not add the basil, oregano, parsley, or savory.

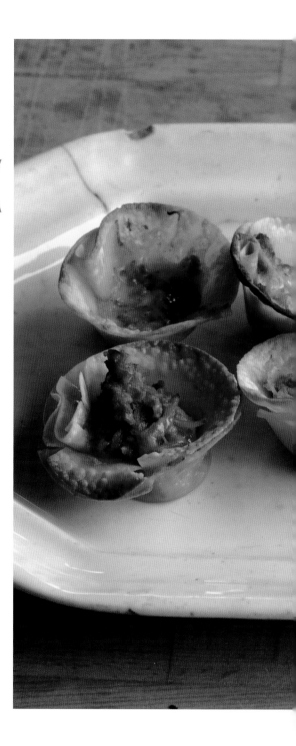

- 1 onion, chopped
- 1 carrot or parsnip, chopped
- 1 beet, chopped
- 1 potato, chopped
- 1 lb. ground beef
- ½ teaspoon salt
- 1 teaspoon dried basil
- ½ teaspoon dried oregano
- ½ teaspoon dried parsley
- ½ teaspoon dried savory
- 1 package round wonton wraps
- ½ cup parmesan cheese

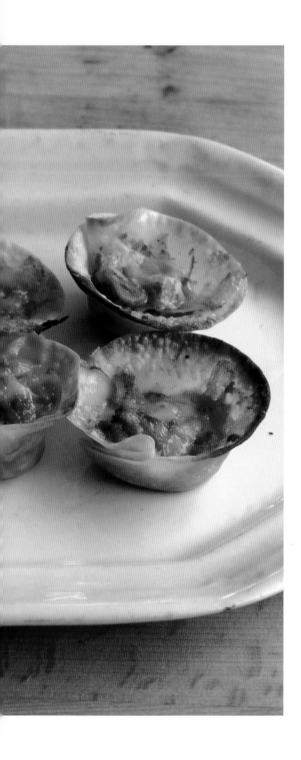

1 Blanch the vegetables by steaming or boiling them.

2 Brown the ground beef with the spices. Mince or mash the blanched vegetables. Mix meat and vegetables together.

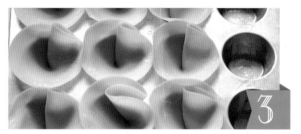

3 Lightly oil a muffin pan or mini-muffin pan. Pinch or fold part of the wonton wrap to make a cone and place the wrapper into the cup of a muffin pan or mini-muffin pan.

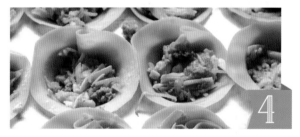

4 Fill the wrapper by spooning in the meat and vegetable mixture. If using a muffin pan, place a second wrapper on top of this and fill the second wrapper. Top with cheese. Repeat until the pan is full.

5 Bake at 350 degrees for 10 minutes or until golden brown around the edges. Serve warm.

No-Fuss Tinfoil Dinners

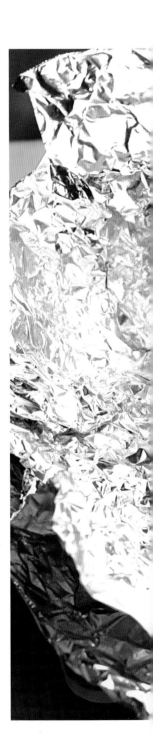

SERVES FOUR

PREPARATION TIME: 15 MINUTES. COOK TIME (OVEN): 50 MINUTES.

Don't want to deal with washing dishes? This meal is for you! You can use the Parma Burger recipe in this book instead of hamburger, if desired.

1 lb. hamburger

2 carrots, diced

2 beets, sliced

1 small summer squash, sliced (optional)

1 large potato, or small potatoes, sliced

salt

pepper

1 You will need three 18-inch-long pieces of tinfoil per person. Take the first sheet and turn it shiny side up on your kitchen counter. Flatten a quarter pound of the hamburger in the center of the tinfoil. Place a quarter of the vegetables on top of the raw meat. If you do not use summer squash, add an ice cube to the vegetables. Salt and pepper the food to taste.

2 Fold opposite sides of the foil to the center. Rotate the tinfoil a quarter-turn and fold in the remaining two sides. You now have a foil-wrapped packet.

3 Turn the wrapped packet upside down and place it in the center of your second piece of tinfoil. Fold the sides as before. Repeat this process with the third piece of tinfoil. Make four individual tinfoil dinner packets in this way.

4 Bake at 350 degrees for 50 minutes, or cook in the coals of a backyard campfire for 20 minutes. Unwrap the foil layers carefully and serve hot.

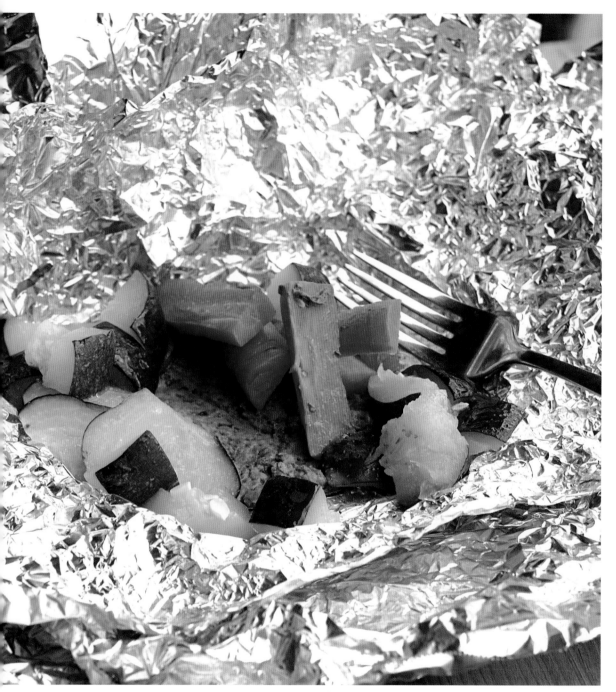

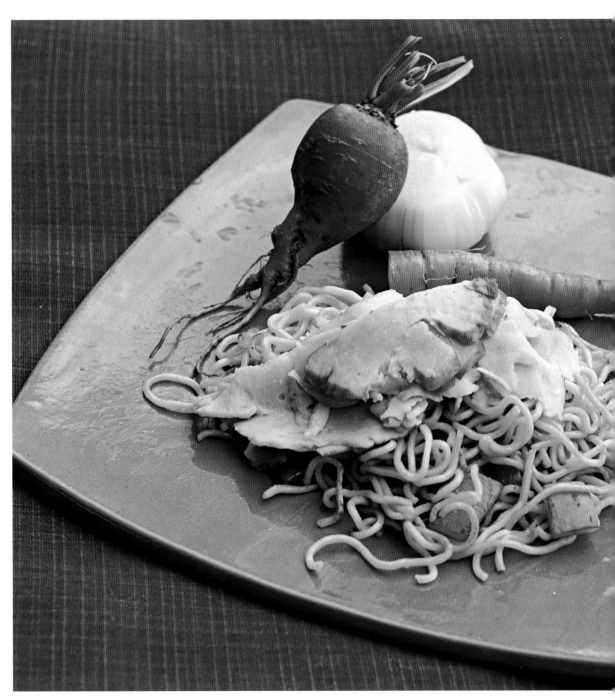

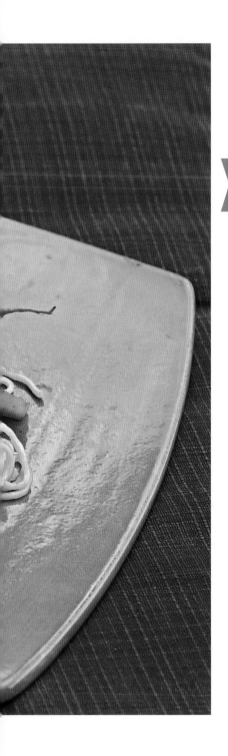

Traditional Japanese Yakisoba

Literally translated, yakisoba means "cooked noodles" in Japanese. When I lived in Japan, this was one of my favorite meals. In addition to being delicious, it takes less than 15 minutes to make from start to finish! Prepared yakisoba noodles are found in the refrigerated section of the vegetable aisle, often near the fresh mushrooms. The noodles come with a packet of powdered seasoning. You will not need that seasoning for this recipe.

2 tablespoons sesame oil

2 carrots or parsnips, diced

1 beets or turnips, diced

1 potato, diced

2 cups of diced Asian cabbage

1 package enoki mushrooms or other favorite mushrooms (optional)

2 pork chops, chicken breasts, or steaks, deboned and thin-sliced

1 package of prepared yakisoba noodles

2 tablespoons water

¼ cup soy sauce

3 teaspoon rice vinegar

1 Heat a wok or heavy pan over medium high heat. Add the oil, vegetables, and meat. Cover the pan. Cook for 5-7 minutes, until the sliced meat is cooked through.

2 Add the noodles, water, soy sauce, and rice vinegar. Cover and cook for 4-5 minutes. Serve hot.

Japanese Gyoza Potstickers

MAKES APPROX. 40 POTSTICKERS
PREPARATION AND COOK TIME: 30 MINUTES

Potstickers are crunchy comfort food at our house. Cooked perfectly, they are crisp on one side and delightfully chewy on the other. Served hot and dipped in gyoza sauce, these are easy to fall in love with. Gyoza is one of a handful of Japanese comfort foods that have taken the western world by storm, and with good reason.

½ onion

1 carrot or parsnips

1 beet

1 potatoes

½ lb. ground pork

1 egg

1 package prepared round wonton wraps

¼ cup water

3 tablespoons olive oil

2 tablespoons water (additional)

1   Blanch the vegetables by steaming or boiling.

2   Mince or mash the blanched vegetables. Mix in the meat and egg.

3   Lightly wet one round wrap with water. Put 1 heaping teaspoon of filling in the center of the wrap. Seal the wrap by using a potsticker press or by pressing the edges closed with the tines of a fork.

4   Put a tablespoon of oil into a frying pan. Heat on medium high. Add about 12 potstickers to the pan and cover with a lid. Cook for 4 minutes. Remove the lid and add 2 tablespoons of water. Immediately replace the lid. Cook for 4–5 minutes until the potstickers are puffy and golden brown on the bottom. Serve hot with gyoza sauce.

Gyoza Sauce

This recipe is per person. This sauce is usually served in a small dipping bowl (available at Asian food stores) at each place setting at the table. Hot potstickers are typically dipped into the sauce using chopsticks. If you are not comfortable using chopsticks, this sauce can be poured over a serving of 10–12 potstickers. The three ingredients in this sauce are not stirred. Simply pour the ingredients into a bowl.

2 teaspoons soy sauce

1 teaspoon sesame oil

1 teaspoon rice vinegar

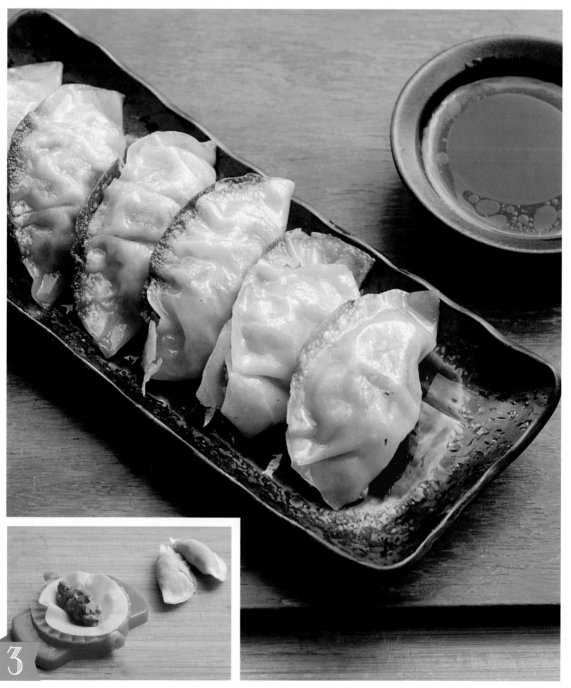

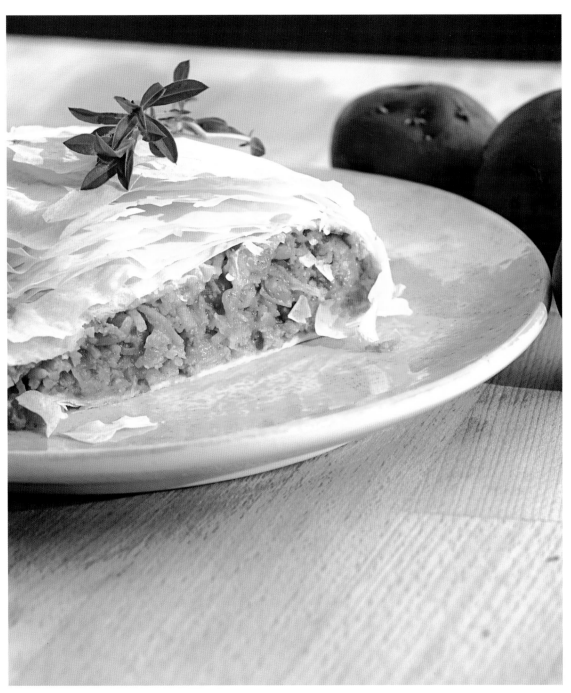

Savory Masala Pastry Roll

Garam Masala is a delicious traditional Indian spice blend that includes coriander, cinnamon, and cumin as its main ingredients. Garam masala is also sometimes just called masala blend and is available in most grocery stores. If you don't have garam masala, substitute a quarter-teaspoon cinnamon, a half-teaspoon coriander, and a quarter-teaspoon of cumin or ground clove.

1 medium potato	1 onion
2 beets	2 carrots
3 tablespoons olive oil	1 handful green beans
½ teaspoon crushed coriander	2 tomatoes
¼ teaspoon ground mustard seed	½-lb. hamburger
¼ teaspoon curry powder	½-lb. Italian sausage or ground pork
1 teaspoon garam masala spice blend	1 roll of prepared filo dough pastry (also called phyllo dough)

1 Shred or grate the root vegetables, either using a food processor or a cheese grater.

2 In a heavy-bottomed pan, heat the oil on medium heat. Add the spices and onion and cook for 4–5 minutes. Add the meat and partial brown it.

3 Add the other vegetables. Chop, blend, or crush the tomatoes and add them to the mix. Cover the pan and cook for ten minutes.

4 On a jelly roll pan or cookie sheet, unroll and lay flat a roll of prepared filo dough. On one half of the dough, spoon the vegetable mix along the length of the dough. Fold the other half of the dough over and pat it down. Bake at 375 degrees for 15 minutes or until golden brown on top. Serve warm.

Kyoto Croquettes

SERVES 4–6

PREPARATION AND COOK TIME: 30 MINUTES

When I lived in the Kyoto area of Japan, these fried potato and vegetable patties were one of my favorite foods. They are sold everywhere: on the street, in every grocery store and deli, and in speciality restaurants. These are patties made of meat and mashed vegetables, which have been breaded and pan-fried. There is nothing like the flavor of a fresh, warm Kyoto Croquette–makes me want to decamp to Japan all over again. This is autumn comfort food at its best. You will notice that this recipe has no spices or herbs in it. This is because it is made with Italian sausage, which contains its own herbs and spices. If you use ground beef, add ¼ teaspoon salt and a pinch of pepper. Called korokke in Japanese, these vegetable/meat patties are also delicious served cold on a hot summer day, and can be made ahead of time for the famous Japanese bento box lunches which are becoming so popular in the U.S. with families looking to eat natural, great-tasting foods.

2 cups steamed or boiled potatoes, mashed

2 cups steamed or boiled root vegetables, mashed (carrots, white or gold beets, parsnips, or turnips).

1 onion, steamed or boiled with the other vegetables

2 eggs

1½ cup seasoned panko bread crumbs

⅓ lb. Italian sausage or ground beef or ground pork

3 tablespoons olive oil

1 Completely mix the vegetables and meat with one egg (reserve the other) and ½ cup of breadcrumbs (reserve the remaining ½ cup).

2 Whisk the remaining egg in a bowl. Form golf-ball-sized rounds of the vegetable and meat mixture. Set each round in the egg, and turn it over so that egg coats two sides of the round. Set each round in the breadcrumbs and flatten with a fork.

3 Heat the olive oil in the frying pan. Brown the croquettes on one side and then the other. Serve warm.

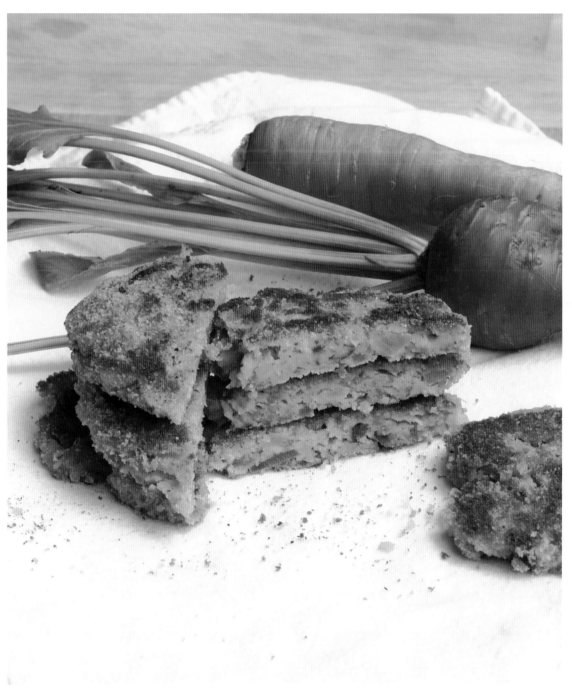

Herbed Summer Squash Coins

SERVES 4–6

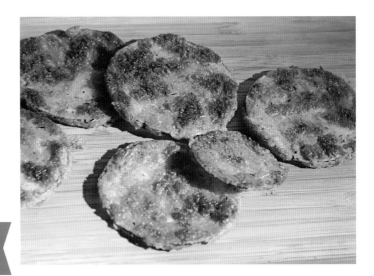

This is hands down one of the most-used recipes in our kitchen in summer. I like making zucchini and yellow squash coins because they are fast, filling, and a great way to use our summer bounty.

1 small summer squash

1 cup whole-wheat flour

¼ teaspoon garlic powder (or more, to taste)

½ teaspoon marjoram

½ teaspoon thyme

½ teaspoon salt

pinch of pepper

1 cup whole milk

2 tablespoons olive oil or cooking oil

1   Slice the squash into no more than a quarter-inch-thick slices. If these coins are larger than a quarter, halve or quarter them.

2   In a plastic food bag, combine flour, herbs, and spices. Dip or sieve the squash coins in milk. No more than a few at a time, drop the wet coins into the bag, twist the bag closed, and shake. Remove the coated coins and continue until you have enough coins to cover the bottom of a larger frying pan in a single layer.

3   Heat the oil in the frying pan and turn the pan to make sure the oil covers the bottom of the pan. Place the breaded squash coins in the oil one at a time, making sure they don't overlap. Cook until golden brown, about 4–5 minutes over medium-high heat.

4   Using a small silicone spatula, turn the coins over. If you are brave and have practiced your Julia Child omelet-tossing technique (and I have!), you can toss the whole pan to turn them over at once. Cook until golden brown on this side. Serve hot.

July Cold Pasta Salad

SERVES 4–6

PREPARATION AND COOK TIME: 15 MINUTES. CHILL TIME (IF DESIRED) 60 MINUTES

There comes a time every summer when hot food just won't do. The heat outside is oppressive. We want food that will fill us up and cool us down. That's when I turn to cold pasta salads.

1 lb. rotini dry pasta

3 medium carrots

2 baby zucchini

2 albino sugar beets

ribs of 4 large chard leaves

½ cup peas or mallow peas

¼ cup cold butter

½ teaspoon marjoram or savory

½ teaspoon salt (optional)

zest of one lemon or lime

1 teaspoon dried basil, or 10 leaves chopped fresh basil

dash of pepper

10 ounces shredded parmesan

1   Bring a large pot of salted water to a boil. Cook pasta, carrots, and beets until tender but firm.

2   In the last minute of cooking the pasta, add the peas, chard ribs, and zucchini.

3   Drain the pasta and vegetables. Add cheese and spices. Grate cold butter with a cheese grater and stir into the pasta. Chill in the fridge if desired. Serve cold.

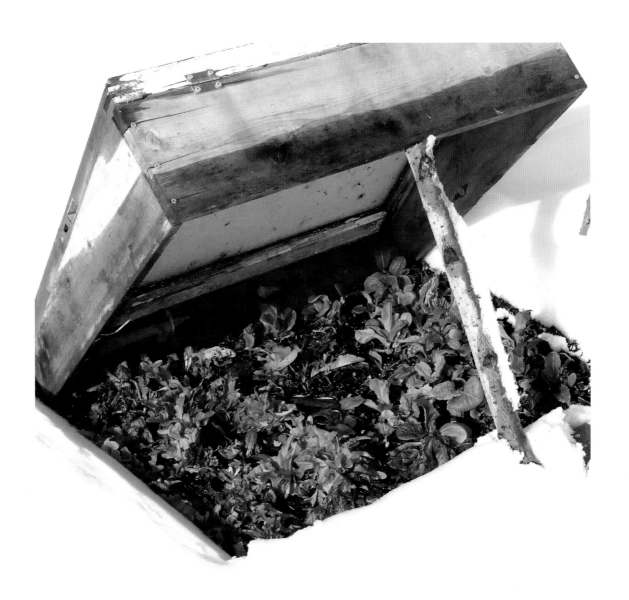

Stir Fry with Summer or Winter Greens

SERVES 4–6

PREPARATION AND COOK TIME: 25 MINUTES

I grow a large amount of fresh greens in our snowy winters using cold frames and a geothermal green-house. Whenever I can come into the house with fresh greens when the world is covered in a blanket of white, we feel healthy, wealthy, and wise. This recipe is one of my favorite winter lunches.

½ medium onion

1 tablespoon olive oil

2 carrots, sliced

1 celery stalk, sliced

canned or fresh pineapple, to taste

1 tablespoon flour (white, wheat, oat, or other)

¼-lb. deli sliced ham

2 cups chopped summer or winter greens (beet greens, cabbage, Chinese cabbage, lettuce)

1 cup rice, cooked

1 Slice the onion thinly. Put the olive oil into a wok or large sauté pan and add the onions on medium heat. Stir onions into the hot oil and allow to cook for two minutes.

2 Stir carrots and celery into onions. Cook for two minutes.

3 Add pineapple. If using canned, add a quarter cup of the juice. Stir in the flour. Add ham and winter greens. Boil for two minutes until greens are hot and wilted. Serve over rice.

Quick Yellow Squash &
Beet Summer Soup

SERVES 4–6 PEOPLE
PREPARATION AND COOK TIME: 10 MINUTES

This soup can be made from start to finish in less than 10 minutes, making it the perfect choice for a hot summer day when you don't want to be over the stove. Use a small yellow squash, usually less than six inches long. However, if you are like me and don't always keep a close eye on your squash, you can simply scoop the seeds out of a larger squash. Don't use a red beet that bleeds color in this soup. Albino Sugar Beets are perfect for this recipe. You can find seeds at SeedRenaissance.com. This recipe can easily be doubled or tripled as needed. If you are using a fresh garden beet, remove the leaves and serve as a side salad with this soup.

1 onion

1 small, tender yellow summer squash

1 large white or gold beet (Albino, Chioggia or Golden beet)

stems of the beet leaves, rinsed

2½ cups whole milk or half-and-half

½ teaspoon salt

½ teaspoon marjoram

pinch of pepper

1   Finely shred the onion, squash, beet, and stems of the beet leaves (not the leaves) with a food processor or by hand using a fine-shred grater. Stems can be minced instead of shredded if desired.

2   Put the shredded vegetables and all remaining ingredients in a pot. Bring to a boil. Cook for three minutes. Serve over crushed ice or chill for 1 hour. Can be served hot or cold.

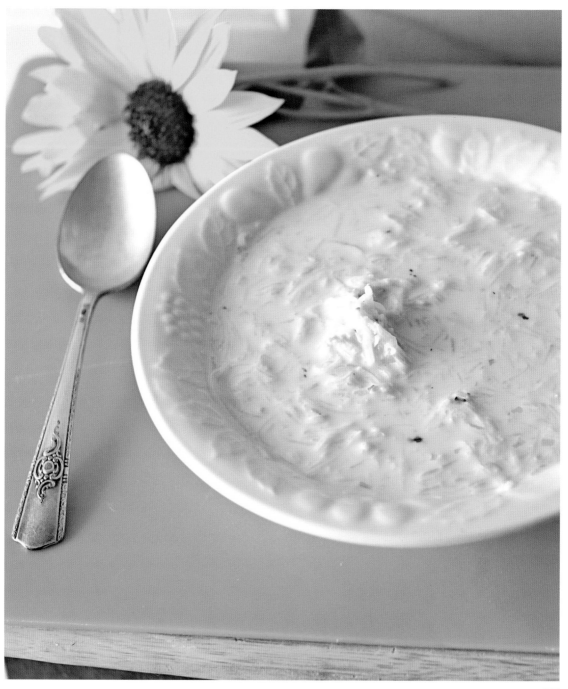

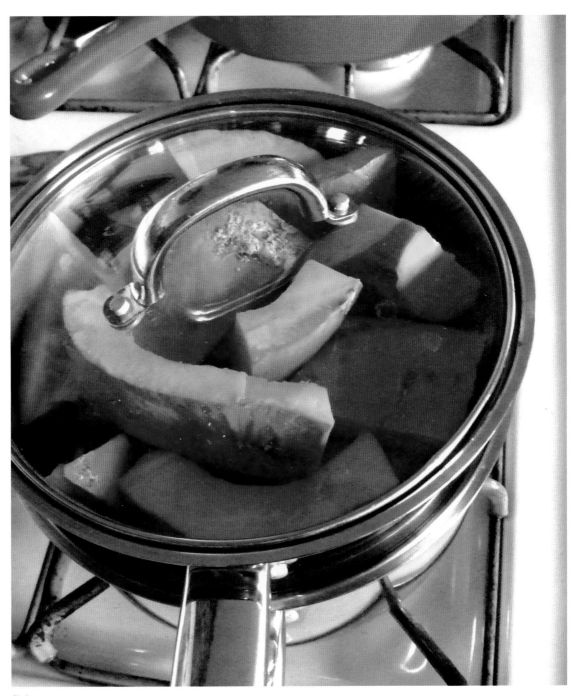

Pumpkin Vichyssoise or "Piping Pie" Soup

SERVES 4–6

PREPARATION AND COOK TIME: 15 MINUTES

This soup is so easy and fast to make, which makes it one of my favorites. In high-end restaurants, this is often served with just a pinch of brown sugar on top, but I don't usually serve it this way at our house. This is a true dual purpose soup. In hot weather, it makes a perfect and flavorful pumpkin version of vichyssoise, which is a fancy word for a cold blended soup. Or in cold weather, serve it hot with Altitude Popovers. When served hot, I like to call this "Piping Pie" soup because it tastes like pumpkin pie.

1 winter pumpkin, (like Mormon Pumpkin, Potimarron, or Waltham Butternut)

2 leeks

1 potato

1 tablespoon butter

1 tablespoon olive oil

½ pint cream

1 cup chicken broth (or more, to taste)

1 teaspoon oat flour

1 tablespoon cinnamon (or more, to taste)

1½ teaspoons nutmeg (or more, to taste)

½ teaspoon salt

1 Remove seeds from the pumpkin, cut into large chunks and steam until tender. Cool until you can handle it with your hands.

2 Dice onions. Sauté in butter and olive oil for 4–5 minutes over medium-low heat, until translucent.

3 In a large measuring cup, mix cream and broth. Remove outer shell from the pumpkin and discard. Pour half of the cream/broth mix into blender, and add half the pumpkin. Blend until smooth. Repeat until all pumpkin is blended. In a large soup pan, mix blended pumpkin, salt and spices, and bring to a boil. Boil for one minute. Serve hot or cold.

Beyond Lettuce:
40 Backyard Salad Ingredients

At our house, salads are any combination of the list below. Sometimes I even use lettuce!

1. Vernal Red Orach. This delicious, easy-to-grow leafy vegetable is a cousin of spinach and is packed with nutrients. The mild, sweet flavor and great purple-red color make it a natural for salad.

2. Mizuna. This Asian green is a winter wonder—it pops up in my geothermal greenhouse despite the cold nights. Grows prolifically and very fast in spring, fall, and winter—even in January—faster and more reliably than other winter greens. Cut at ground level and it will grow back over and over. And it's just fun to look at and it with its frisée leaves. Bright green. Great for salads.

3. Komatsuna. Asian greens like this one have been surging in popularity in the U.S. in the last couple of years.

4. Sunchoke. Also called Jerusalem artichoke. This is basically a sunflower plant that produces an edible, potato-like root. Sunchokes are ready to harvest as soon as the ground thaws in spring. Slice or dice them for salad.

5. Purslane. Wherever you live, you are likely to have purslane growing near you. I eat this almost everyday of summer, straight from the garden. Purslane is my favorite among all the wild edibles, with a flavor like crunchy romaine topped with lemon vinaigrette. The light citrus flavor is natural.

6. Baby Chinese cabbage. Michihili is the variety I grow in my garden. The plants get huge—the leaves can be up to two feet long—but the young leaves are particularly good for salad.

7. Caleb's Fine Fettle Greens. These winter greens are a natural, non-hybrid cross that I created on my property between rutabaga and Siberian kale to make stable, cabbage-y, crunchy winter greens that can be harvested all winter without any protection. We eat it all winter long. I particularly like it because it is substantive and crunchy and produces huge leaves, even in sub-zero weather!

8. Beet greens. The leaves of beets are great in salads whether young or mature. The smooth leaves give substance to a salad. These are in almost every salad we eat at our house, year-round, thanks to the greenhouse.

9. Baby turnip greens. The young leaves of the turnip are tender and flavorful, but after about 45 days, they become hairy and less edible. Don't take too many young leaves from any one plant or you could keep the plant from forming a turnip later in summer.

10. "Nocturnal" or "Sleeping" Beet Greens. When mature beets are boxed for winter storage, they will slowly begin to grow leaves in the dark. These leaves are tender and beautiful, and are fantastic in salad. Even in the dark, beet greens develop some red stems in the leaves, just as they do in the summer garden. This makes them look even better in a fresh winter salad. Better yet, if you cut these naturally blanched leaves, they will quickly grow back. Best of all, the flavor of the beet will be unaffected and you can still eat them as normal. Turnips, dandelions, and chicory also produce nocturnal greens. For more information, see my Backyard Winter Gardening book.

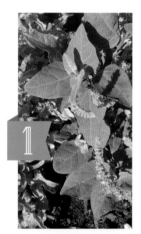

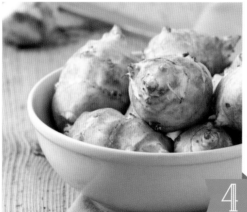

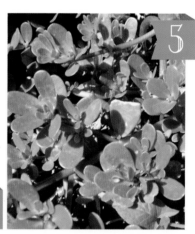

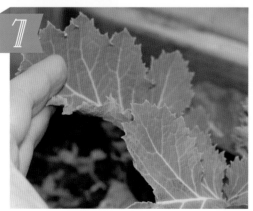

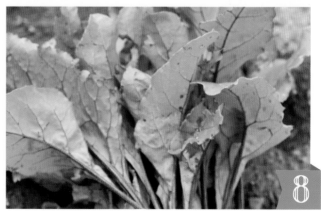

11. Pea shoot tips. The tendrils and leaves from the tips of pea shoots taste exactly like garden peas, and make a great addition to salads.

12. Pea flowers. These quarter-sized blossoms come in shades of white and purple, and look great in salads.

13. Tout-mange pea pods. Tout-mange is a French term that means "eat-all". Most varieties of peas taste good when the pods are young and have not filled yet. My favorite for this is Golden Sweet Snow Peas, available at SeedRenaissance.com, which is my seed company.

14. Baby cabbage leaves. After you have harvested the head from early varieties of cabbage such as Danish Ballhead, it is not unusual for the plants to put out shoots with small baby cabbages. These small leaves are great for salad.

15. Finely shredded cabbage. Shredding cabbage releases this vegetable's natural sweetness. Sometimes I like to have a salad with made of nothing but shredded cabbage and vinaigrette.

16. Chives. These thin shoots add a burst of onion flavor to salad.

17. Chive flowers. These purple spheres add heat and color to any salad. Break the flower into individual florets and sprinkle them sparingly over your salad.

18. Garlic chives. Traditionally used in Asian cuisine, this tall grass tastes almost exactly like garlic. Garnish a salad with the chopped leaves, especially if you are using a creamy garlic dressing.

19. Egyptian Walking onion shoots. These are a great substitute for green onions in autumn and spring. Use just like you would green onions.

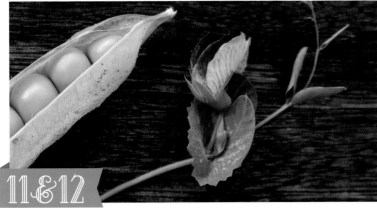

11 & 12

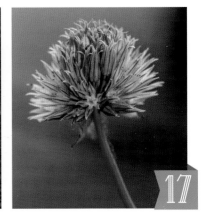

17

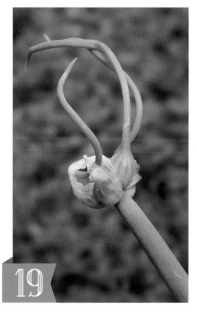

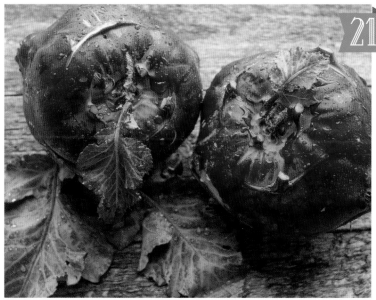

20. Long carrot peels. I like some crunch in my salads--crunch gives salad substance, slows me down as I eat, and makes me feel full. My all-time favorite way to add crunch, and color, to a salad is to use a vegetable peeler to turn a whole carrot into a pile of long peels, and then toss these into the salad.

21. Kohlrabi. Kohlrabi is a root vegetable with a broccoli flavor. Slices, pieces, or especially julienned slices are a great addition to salad.

22. Kale chips. Kale chips are made by coating kale leaves lightly in olive oil and sea salt and baking them in a 350-degree oven for a few minutes. You might not think this would be a delicious treat, but you would be very wrong-- the surprising savory flavor is nothing short of addicting. If you can keep from eating them all straight out of the oven, kale chips make a great garnish for salad, or a substitute for croutons when broken up into pieces.

23. Kale leaves. Not just for baking, raw kale leaves are a good addition to any salad. To toss them in, roll the leaves up and chop roughly with a knife.

24. Broccoli raab. The loose florets of broccoli that don't form a head are called raab. Raab often forms after the main head of broccoli has been cut. They are a chewy addition to any salad.

25. Cauliflower florets. Who needs salad? Just dip these in ranch dressing and what else do you need? But if you must have a salad, these bring crunch to the dish.

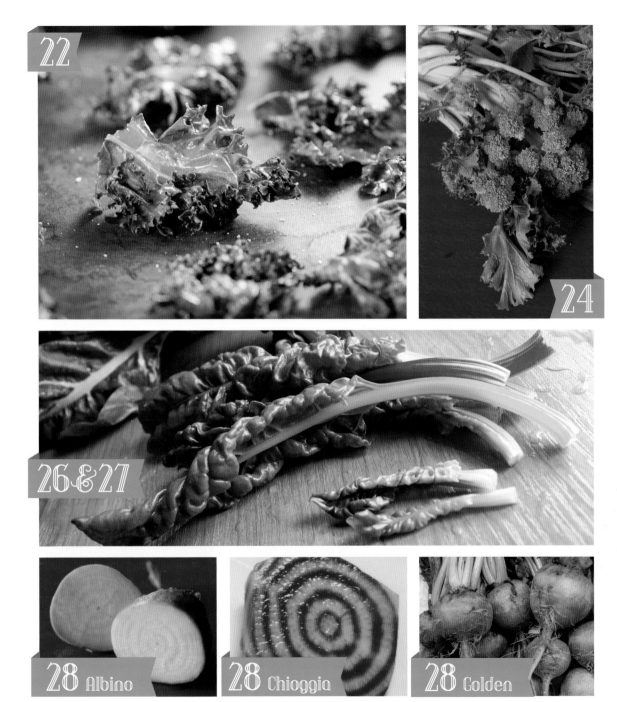

22

24

26&27

28 Albino

28 Chioggia

28 Golden

26. Swiss chard leaves. I prefer "Bright Lights," which include yellow, red, white, green, and pink leaves. Roll the leaves and roughly chop them to add color and flavor to a tossed salad.

27. Swiss chard ribs. In Italy, chard ribs––the center stem of the leaf, including the stalk–are widely used as a substitute for celery to add flavor to soups and tomato sauce. Chard ribs are much easier to grow than celery, more nutritious than celery, and have great crunch and flavor. Add them to a salad just like they were cut celery.

28. Sliced beets. Sliced beets, especially non-bleeding varieties such as Albino, Chioggia, or Golden beets, bring real flavor to a salad. Or try them pickled.

29. Parsnip coins. Parsnips seem to be rarely eaten these days in the United States, which is a mistake because they are great! They have a flavor all their own, and the flavor is great. Parsnips are a white carrot-like root and can be sliced into coins for any salad.

30. Spinach. Spinach is an old friend to salad. I prefer the baby leaves, especially of the America Spinach variety.

31. Sweet basil. This herb, with its big, tender leaves full of flavor, is a mainstay of kitchens everywhere, but not used raw in salads as often as it should be. A burst of flavor!

32. Collard greens. Collard greens are so easy to grow and have edible leaves almost every day of the year, even deep into winter. They add substance when they are tossed into a salad.

33. Red choi sum. This is a beautiful Asian green that grows quickly and has a mild flavor. As you guessed by the name, this leafy green adds a pop of red to green salads. Color is something I really feel the lack of when it is missing from my salad plate.

34. Tai sai. Tai sai is another fast-growing, easy leaf vegetable with a mild flavor that compliments other salad greens. Tai sai is also great for harvesting in autumn and spring.

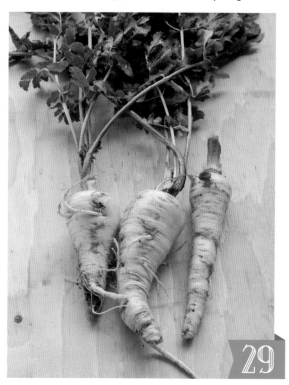

29

35. Lemon balm. For a bit of citrusy surprise, add leaves of lemon balm, which is also called melissa. These fragrant leaves bring big lemon flavor.

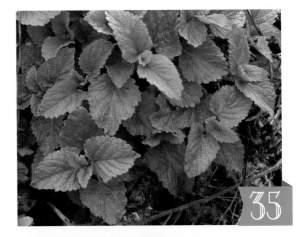

36. Mallow peas. Everyone has had garden peas in a salad, but few people have taken advantage of mallow peas. This wild edible is also called the cheese-it plant, or cheese plant, and many children remember eating it straight from the backyard in childhood. Mallow peas are at their peak at the height of summer, after most peas have gone starchy. I grow these in my winter greenhouse too.

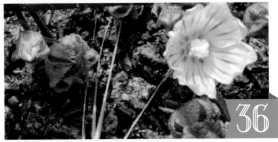

37. Diced hard boiled egg. A classic. Of course they taste and look best if you are lucky enough to have backyard hens.

38. Osaka purple mustard greens. These bring unparalleled color to a salad, but beware, they also bring a horseradish-like heat. If you like horseradish, you will love these greens.

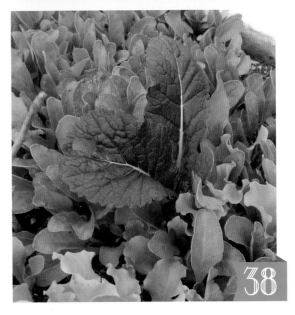

39. Spring dandelion greens. Pick them before the flowers open and they won't have the hot flavor that comes after the flowers.

40. Dandelion crowns. The crown is the part of the plant where the leaves come out of the top of the root. Dandelion crowns are great raw and sautéed.

Pumpkin Spinach Curry Stir Fry

SERVES 4–6

PREPARATION AND COOK TIME: 30 MINUTES

I created this recipe at the request of my wife, who wanted us to eat more stir-fry with our fresh garden vegetables, especially in winter.

1 large onion

1 tablespoon butter

1½ tablespoon olive oil

2 cups (roughly) pumpkin, butternut, or other winter squash

leaves from 3 sprigs fresh thyme OR 1 teaspoon dried thyme

2–3 carrots

½ cup water

½ cup cashews raw or salted (do not add salt below if you use salted cashews)

1 cup chopped mushrooms

½ teaspoon salt

½ teaspoon curry powder or more to taste

¼ teaspoon ground clove

½ teaspoon ground turmeric

¼ teaspoon ground nutmeg

1 cup water

1 handful fresh spinach

2 cups cooked spaghetti squash OR rice or other grains (wheat, quinoa, etc.)

1 Sauté onions with butter and olive oil over low heat. While they cook slowly, cut up your raw pumpkin into wedges roughly two inches long and a third-inch thick.

2 Add the pumpkin and thyme to the onions to cook. Turn carrots into peels but do not add yet. Once the carrots are peeled, add a half-cup of water to your onions and pumpkin and cover. Let this steam for about five minutes until water evaporates. Remove lid, stir.

3 Add cashews, mushrooms, carrots, salt, curry, cloves, turmeric, nutmeg, and one cup water. Cook 3-4 minutes, stirring. Pumpkin will begin to fall apart as you stir and form a sauce. Once the sauce is formed, serve topped with fresh, raw spinach and enjoy!

Jardin Au Gratin

SERVES 4–6

PREPARATION AND COOK TIME: 25 MINUTES

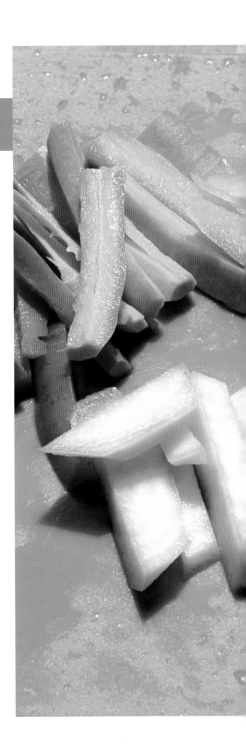

The amount of onion called for in this recipe may seem like a lot, but once you try it, you will realize it is not. In French, au gratin means "with grating". Not only is this recipe fast, but it's also mouth-watering. It's one of our favorites. We usually make it without the bacon, because cooking the bacon doubles the time it takes to make this recipe, but if you have some leftover cooked bacon, this is a great recipe for it.

1 medium potato per person

1 carrot per person

½ onion, diced per person

1 large button mushroom per person

½ cup grated cheese per person

½ teaspoon ground sage per person

salt, pepper to taste

crumbled bacon to taste (optional)

1 Grate the potatoes and carrots. In a mixing bowl, mix the vegetables with the remaining ingredients.

2 Cook your vegetable mixture in a nonstick frying pan, using a spatula to press the mixture flat. Cook over medium-low heat until the cheese bubbles in the center. On our gas stove, the settings go from zero, which is off, to 10, which is high. I cook this on the 3 heat setting for ten minutes on one side, then use a spatula to loosen the vegetable cake and then flip it over. I cook it for another ten minutes and serve warm.

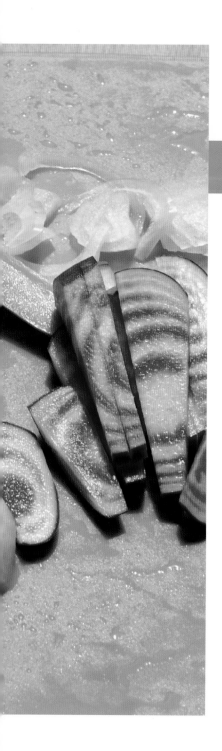

Leek, Beet Greens, and Bacon Stir Fry

SERVES 4–6

PREPARATION AND COOK TIME: 25 MINUTES

6 slices bacon julienned (julienne means cut into matchstick size pieces)

6-10 Chinese cabbage leaves, julienned

large handful of young beet greens and stems, chopped

2 medium beet, julienned

2 large leek, diced

2 medium carrot, julienned

2 tablespoons soy sauce

2 teaspoons rice vinegar

1 teaspoon brown sugar

2 cups cooked rice

1   Cook julienned bacon. Add carrots, beets, and leeks, and sauté until tender.

2   Add Chinese cabbage and beet greens and sauté for one minute. Add soy sauce, vinegar, and brown sugar. Cook for an additional 30 seconds and then remove from heat. Serve over warm rice. Serves four.

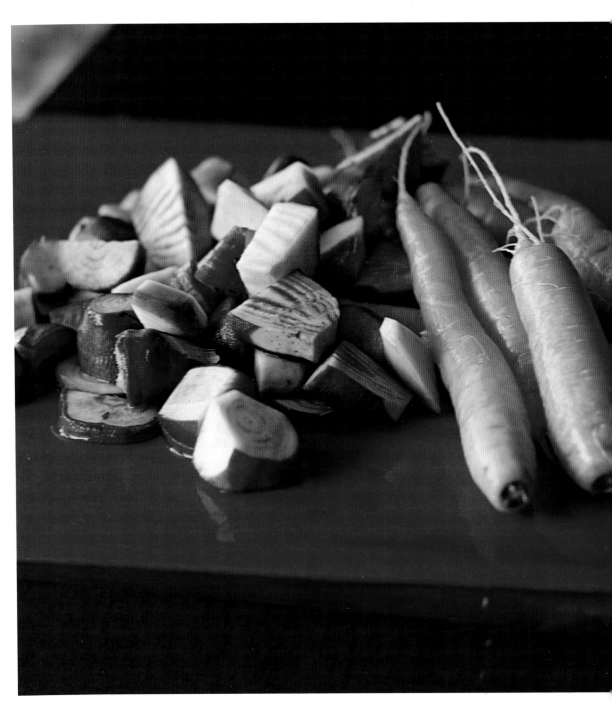

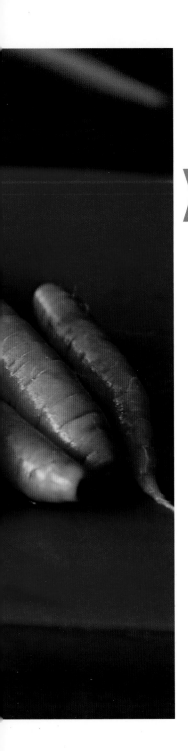

Herb-Crusted Roasted Vegetables

SERVES 4–6
PREPARATION TIME: 20 MINUTES. COOK TIME: 60 MINUTES

There is something about deep snow and blizzardy winds that make us want to eat hearty food at our house. This recipe can be made to stand alone, or to be cooked with a small roast in the center of the pan, or even cooked with pork chops or steaks at the bottom of the pan.

2 potatoes

3 carrots

2 beets

2 turnips

Potimarron or Mormon squash
  (or any winter squash)

2 onions

1 tablespoon olive oil

1 tablespoon ground sage

½ tablespoon rosemary

¼ teaspoon ground pepper

½ teaspoon salt

¼ teaspoon thyme

1 Cut the vegetables into large chunks, about the size of a quarter. Coat them in the olive oil and fill a large casserole dish with them. Top with the herbs. Cover the pan.

2 Bake at 400 degrees for 60 minutes. Serve warm.

Optional Sprinkle parmesan cheese over the vegetables just as they come out of the oven.

Fresh Tomato Clove Stew

SERVES 6–8

PREPARATION AND COOK TIME: 40 MINUTES

This is one of my all-time favorite autumn meals. I created this stew because I love the flavor of cloves. (We also love to drink clove-based wassail cider at our house every Christmas.) Because of the cloves, this stew has a flavor like no other tomato stew you've ever tasted–it's savory for miles.

Because this stew always disappears rapidly, I make it in big batches, as you will see below. You can freeze this stew if you have leftovers, or you can eat it for several days–this is one of those rare stews that actually tastes better the second day, as the potatoes take up the flavor of the tomatoes and clove. You can use whatever potatoes you have on hand to make this, but butterball varieties take this stew from excellent to exceptional.

The reason this recipe is a stew and not a soup is because there is no water at all in this recipe. If you choose to use a beef stock instead of bouillon granules, you will need to cook the stew at least 40 minutes longer to reduce the water. This stew goes especially well with a slice of the Roasted Red Bell Pepper & Asiago Sourdough in my cookbook The Art of Baking With Natural Yeast, *which I co-authored with Melissa Richardson.*

10 cups fresh tomato purée

4 cups small diced butter-variety potatoes

1 cup diced ribs of Swiss chard

¼ cup finely diced leaves of fresh parsley

¼ cup finely diced leaves of fresh basil

¼ cup olive oil

1 medium onion finely diced

1 leek finely diced

2 cups fresh corn, cut off the cob

2 tablespoons all-natural beef bouillon granules

½ teaspoon salt

1 teaspoon ground cloves

1 Place the tomato purée in a 4-quart or large pot over medium heat. Add the potatoes, ribs of Swiss chard, parsley, and basil, and bring to a simmer.

2 In a frying pan, heat the olive oil over medium heat. Add the onion and leek and cook in the oil until soft, about three minutes. Add the corn and cook for another five minutes, until the sugar in the corn begins to caramelize. Add the corn mixture to the tomato mixture.

3 Add the remaining ingredients and cook until the potatoes are cooked through. Serve hot.

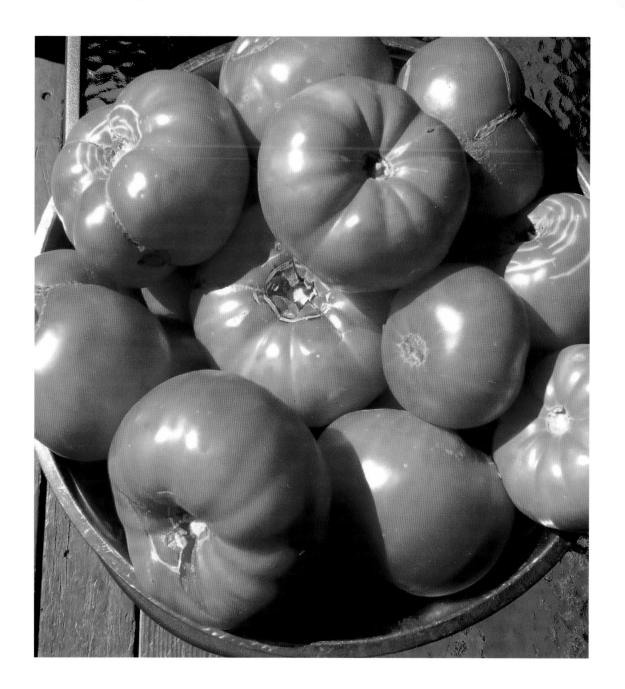

Christmas Eve Stew

SERVES 6–8

PREPARATION AND COOK TIME: 30 MINUTES

Every Christmas Eve, we do two things at our house. First, we go to our church for a short devotional, after which every single man, woman, and child is given a brown paper bag with an orange, peanuts, and a few candies. This tradition began seventy years ago, at the height of the Great Depression, when Alpine, Utah, was a small town, and families were looking at quite a bleak Christmas. The Burgess family owned an orchard (they still do), and they scrounged up some apples and a bit of candy and gave them to everyone in the town at church on Christmas Eve. There is no more perfect way to celebrate Christmas Eve, and we never miss it.

After the annual devotional, we come home through the blowing snow to our scratch stew. In recent years, our stew has been completely self-sufficient. The carrots, potatoes, and onions are from our garden. The beef is from our pasture. Delicious, and wholly self-sufficient. This self-provident stew is probably a close replica of what the original folk here would have eaten on Christmas Eve during the Great Depression. Certainly most of the farming families (it was an all-farming community then) would have used their own vegetables in their winter soup, and most likely their own protein too. Going to a Christmas devotional, having our brown paper sack with an orange and peanuts, and eating self-provident stew feels like a humble and appropriate way to remember those who came before us and their sacrifices.

1 small rump roast, raw, diced

4 medium potatoes, diced

4 carrots, sliced

2 beets, diced

2 onions, chopped

¼ cup dried basil

1 teaspoon salt

¼ teaspoon pepper

4 cups all-natural beef stock or homemade vegetable stock

1 Put the meat, vegetables, and spices into a large soup pot. Pour the stock over the ingredients. Fill the pot with enough water to cover the ingredients by about half an inch.

2 Bring the pot to a boil. Cover the pan. Turn the heat to medium-low. Cook until vegetables are tender, about 20 minutes. Serve warm.

Christmas Wassail

Another Christmas Eve tradition is to serve Wassail all evening as we gather with friends and family. The word wassail is said to come from the Old English "waes hail" meaning "be you healthy." Wassail was a traditional ceremony performed in rural England by fruit growers to bless the health of their orchards. In modern times, wassail has come be to the name of a mulled cider served especially at Christmas. We have never celebrated a Christmas Eve without it. It makes the whole house smell like Christmas.

1 gallon apple cider

1 tablespoon whole cloves

1 teaspoon lemon zest

1 teaspoon orange zest

2 cinnamon sticks

1 Put the cider and spices into a large pot on the stove and heat until warm. Turn the temperature to the lowest possible setting, and let the wassail steep as long as you like. The flavor deepens as the evening goes on.

Note Some traditional recipes add alcohol to the wassail, but we do not. Other versions of this recipe call for 2 cups of orange juice or even a cup of lemon juice. You can also add ginger and nutmeg if you wish. Some people stick the whole cloves into an orange and a lemon and put them in the cider. There are also commercial wassail spice blends available. Because I cannot resist, here is a 500-year-old traditional wassailing verse:

"Wassail the trees, that they may bear
You many a plum, and many a pear:
For more or less fruits they will bring,
As you do give them wassailing."
–Robert Herrick (1591-1674)
"Ceremonies of Christmas Eve"

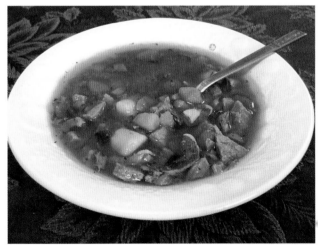

Parma Burgers

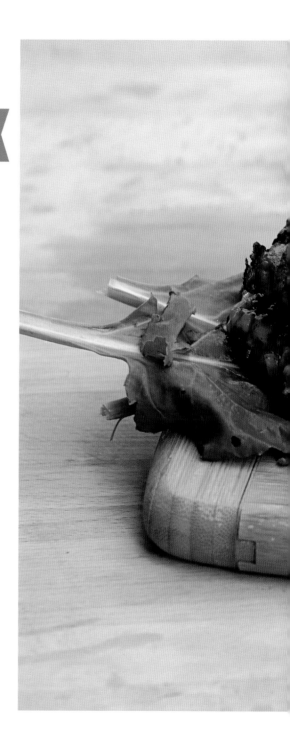

One of our family's favorite quick meals is burgers and fries. We grow our own beef on our little acre-and-a-third homestead, so we usually have hamburger close at hand. Making a great burger differentiates someone who loves to cook and someone who cooks. This recipe makes 4–5 burgers and can be doubled.

Throughout this book, I included recipes that require few if any ingredients outside of vegetables, herbs, spices, and proteins. In this recipe you will find a secret ingredient that I buy at the grocery store (all natural beef bouillon). In addiction, This recipe calls for a fresh onion, minced. Chopped onions are too large for hamburgers. Because minced onions expose more surface area of the onion, they impart more flavor.

1 lb. ground beef (or ground sirloin, half-beef, or half ground pork)

1 minced onion

½ cup shredded Parmesan cheese

1 tablespoon organic, all-natural beef bouillon

¼ teaspoon salt

dash of pepper (white pepper preferably)

1 Mix all ingredients thoroughly.

2 Form patties and cook in a frying pan.

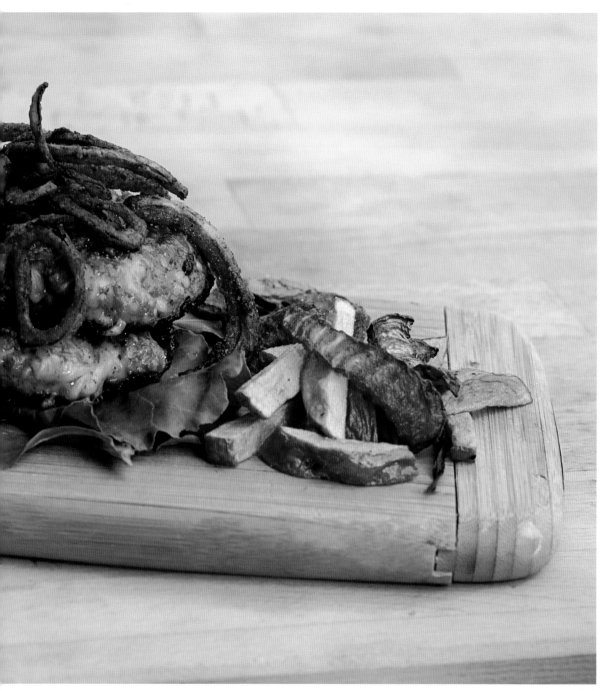

Sweet Color Fries

I have never, ever made burgers without also making fries and onion rings to go with them. White potatoes make the grade only in an emergency. I like to use carrots in yellow, white, red, purple, and even orange. As explained in my first Forgotten Skills book, orange carrots are actually a late-comer to the vegetable world. Carrots started as white and purple. You can find an array of heirloom color carrot varieties at SeedRenaissance.com, or go to your local farmers market. In addition to carrots, I make fries from sweet potatoes and Chioggia or Gold beets, but any type of beet that does not bleed red juice will work. When I do use potatoes, I'm partial to the Mountain Rose variety, which are red inside and stay red when cooked. What can I say—I like color. Colored vegetables tend to have more nutrients than their white-fleshed siblings.

olive oil

Potatoes (optional)

Sweet Potatoes

carrots

beets

salt

1   Heat the oil. Note that olive oil smokes at a lower temperature than canola oil or vegetable oil. Unless you watch your fries like a hawk, the olive oil will smoke, so turn on your smoke hood. Oil is generally hot enough for deep frying when the surface of the oil begins to glisten intensely and look "watery." Test a small piece of potato. If the oil sizzles and boils instantly and intensely enough to cover the potato for a few seconds, the oil is hot enough.

2   Slice the potatoes, carrots, beets, and sweet potatoes into fries. Dry the raw fries in a cotton cloth or paper towels. This step is critical for two reasons. First, it makes the fries crunchier. Second, removing the natural moisture on the cut potatoes means your oil will not spatter.

3   Ladle the raw fries into the oil and cook until golden brown. Remove from oil, salt immediately, and drain on paper towels.

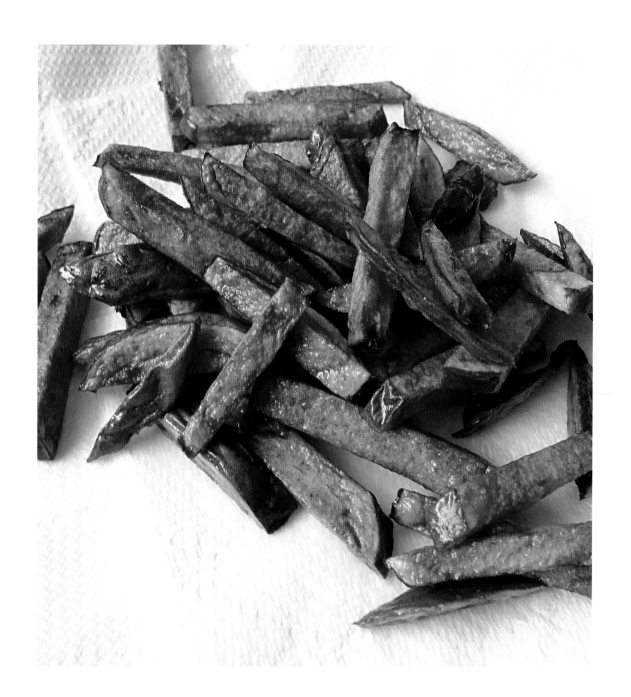

Irish Breaded Onion Rings

PREPARATION AND COOK TIME: 10 MINUTES

Homemade onion rings are actually an ancient comfort food of Ireland and Scotland, where my ancestors emigrated from, which must explain why I have always loved them. These literally take less than 5 minutes to make from scratch. I usually make them after I make Sweet Color Fries because some of the breading flour for the onion rings comes off into the oil and I don't want flour particles on the fries.

Caution: Thin-sliced onion rings cook "in a flash" compared to Sweet Color Fries (see previous recipe), which means that onion rings cook in 20–30 seconds. Be prepared to remove them as soon as they turn golden, otherwise they will burn. You'll also notice that this recipe calls for whole-wheat flour. White flour will do in a pinch. If you are not eating wheat unless it has been treated with natural yeast, skip the milk and flour in this recipe and use natural yeast, thinned slightly with milk, in their place. (For information on natural yeast, see The Art of Baking with Natural Yeast, *coauthored by Melissa Richardson and myself.)*

2 onions	½ teaspoon salt
1 cup whole milk	pinch of pepper
1 cup whole-wheat flour	¼ teaspoon garlic powder (or more, to taste)

1 Begin heating your cooking oil.

2 In a plastic food bag, combine flour, salt, pepper, and garlic powder. Slice the onions as thinly as you can and break the slices into individual rings with your fingers. Dip them in milk. Drop the wet onions into the bag, no more than a few at a time, and shake the bag. When the onions are coated with flour, remove them from the bag, shaking off excess flour.

3 Once your cooking oil has heated, turn the heat down to medium-low. Be aware that thin-sliced onion rings cook very quickly. Ladle into the hot oil and remove when golden brown. Drain on paper towels. Immediately salt lightly and serve hot.

Italian Pasta & Chard Soup

This hearty soup has a secret ingredient: the ribs (center stem) of Swiss chard leaves, which are often used in place of celery in traditional Italian cooking. Only the stems are used in this recipe. To prepare the chard, simply remove the leaves by cutting away the leaf with the tip of a knife, first up one side of the stem and then down the other. To avoid being wasteful, chop or chiffonade the chard leaves and serve them with vinaigrette for an appetizer salad.

2 onions

3 tablespoons olive oil

2 tablespoons butter

1 medium potato

6-7 large Swiss chard stems

2 carrots

1 pint tomato sauce

2 cups hot water

3 tablespoons ground oregano

2 tablespoons ground basil

salt, pepper to taste

1 box penne or rotini pasta

sweet Italian sausage (optional)

1 Dice the onions and sauté them in the oil and butter for 10 minutes in a large, covered soup pot. Meanwhile, julienne the potato and carrots, and finely chop the chard stems. Add to the pot, stir, and cook for an additional 10 minutes.

2 Add tomato sauce, hot water, and the rest of the ingredients. Bring to a boil and cook for exactly 7 minutes. It is important not to overcook the pasta, or it will become mushy. Top with Parmesan, mizithra, or other Italian cheese.

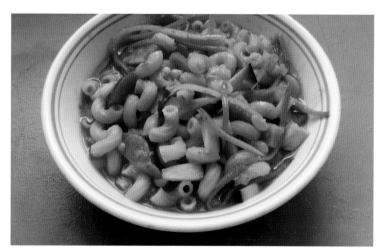

Altitude Popovers

SERVES 4-6

PREPARATION TIME: 5 MINUTES. COOK TIME: 35 MINUTES.

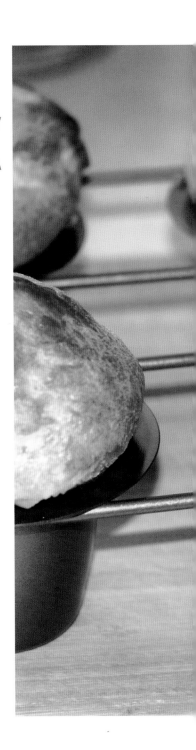

I published the traditional recipe for English Popovers in my book Trouble's On The Menu. I have used that recipe for more than 20 years, but it has never been as light and fluffly as popovers made closer to sea level. A year ago, I stumbled upon a chef, Bob Ballantyne of The Cowboy and The Rose Catering in Grand Rapids, Colorado, who had become frustrated with not being able to make the kind of light and fluffy popovers he yearned for while living in the mountain tops. He spent months developing a recipe for popovers baked at altitude. I'm so grateful! If you don't live at altitude, refer to the original recipe in Trouble's On The Menu.

This recipe is fantastic and I use it exclusively now. I've changed the recipe a bit because the original recipe made too much batter, which made my popovers raise too high, with chunks falling into the bottom of the stove and burning. If you've never had a popover before, think of them as hollow biscuits. They are traditionally eaten with gravy at the dinner table, but they are just as good if they are served hot with butter or homemade jam or jelly. My stepdaughter likes to eat them with syrup. We eat these a lot at our house–as soon as you taste them, you'll understand why. Make sure you serve them straight out of the oven–they are not as good when they are cold. Poke a hole in the top of each muffin before serving to vent the steam, otherwise you might burn your fingers.

1 cup milk

3 eggs

1 cup bread flour

1 tablespoon melted butter or olive oil

½ teaspoon salt

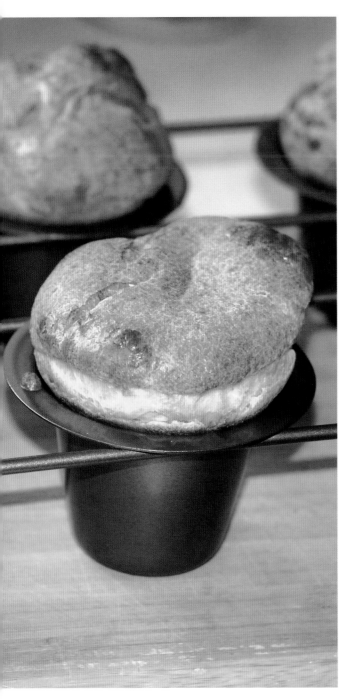

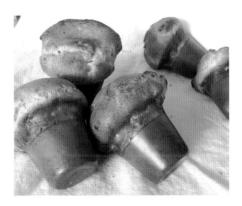

1 Put milk and eggs in a glass bowl without mixing and put in microwave for 60 seconds to warm them slightly. Your popovers will "pop" up higher if you warm the milk and eggs like this.

2 After removing the bowl from the microwave, mix in flour, oil, and salt. Mix until just barely incorporated–do not overmix! Don't use an electric mixer. I use a Danish dough hook, but you could use a whisk or even just a fork. The batter will be a little lumpy, and this is how it should be. Pour batter into popover cups or muffin tins, filling each two-thirds full. If you fill any more than this, they will very likely overtop the pan when baking and fall into the bottom of your oven–take my word for it. Bake at 400 degrees for 35 minutes. Serve hot with butter or homemade jam, syrup, or the traditional English way with gravy or roast drippings!

Carrot Tonkatsu

SERVES 4–6

PREPARATION AND COOK TIME: 30 MINUTES

2 cups of rice, cooked

4-6 breaded chicken breasts or pork chops

1 Egg

1 cup breadcrumbs

1 large or two small onions

2 large carrots

1 tablespoon olive oil

1 tablespoon butter

1 tablespoon olive oil (another)

1 tablespoon flour (whole wheat, oat, or white)

1 cup milk

½ teaspoon curry powder (or to taste)

½ teaspoon Chinese Five Spice Blend (available in most grocery stores)

½ teaspoon turmeric

1 Cook the rice. At the same time, coat your chicken breasts or pork chops with whisked egg and coat with herbed breadcrumbs. Cook in a tablespoon of oil over medium heat in a frying pan and set aside to cool.

2 In covered pan, sauté the onions and carrots together in the olive oil and butter for ten minutes, or until the carrots are tender.

3 Push the vegetables out of the center of the pan to clear a space for the second tablespoon of olive oil and the flour. Stir them together in the center of the pan and cook for 90 seconds. Stir in the remaining ingredients, bringing the milk to a boil. Turn off heat and spoon curry over rice. Slice breaded chicken or pork chops into ½-inch slices and serve over the curry and rice.

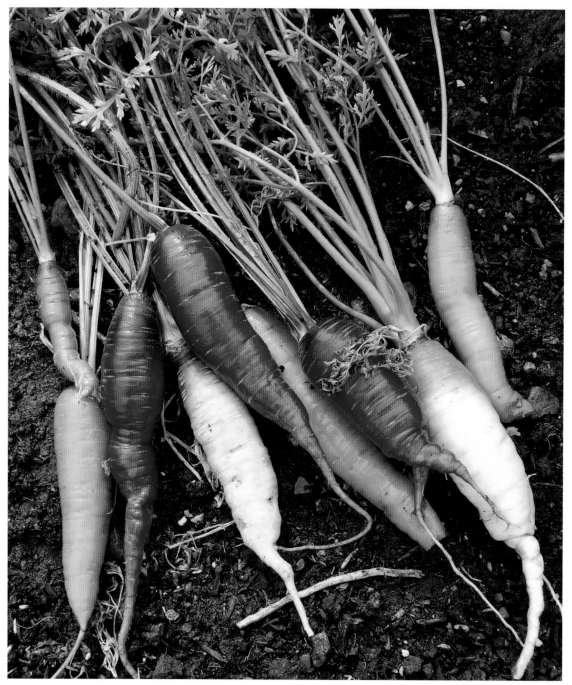

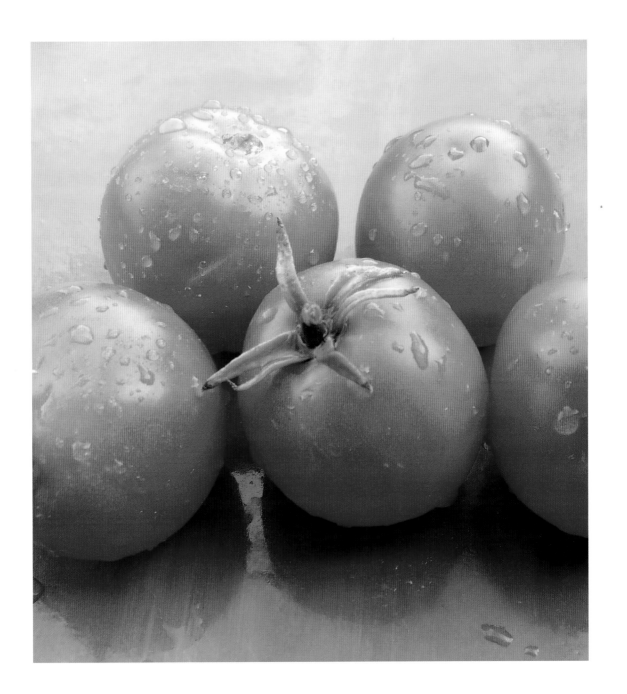

Caleb Warnock

Tomato Pumpkin Curry

SERVES 4–6

PREPARATION AND COOK TIME: 30 MINUTES

This is a great recipe for autumn or winter, and a perfect way to use garden pumpkins and winter squashes, if you have them. In the recipe, I give you the option of using your tomatoes diced or puréed. I prefer them puréed, but it works either way. Note that there is no salt in this recipe--you won't need it or miss it with the other spices. Masala is an Indian blend of ground, dried roasted spices. You can add more if you like your curry fiery. Masala is now available in most grocery stores. Turmeric is a root that is a cousin of ginger and is one of the best health foods around. It is also the spice that gives yellow mustard its color. Turmeric is great for joint pain and is anti-inflammatory. According to the National Institutes of Health, research shows that "tumeric might help improve an upset stomach" and "can reduce the pain caused by osteoarthritis of the knee. In one study, turmeric worked about as well as ibuprofen for reducing pain." One more note: I don't list meat in the recipe below, but sometimes I do add meat protein. You could use pork, beef, chicken, or even bacon–they all work great.

1 onion puréed or finely minced

4 carrots puréed or finely minced

1 tablespoon butter

1 tablespoon olive oil

3 cups water

3 tomatoes, diced or 24 oz. tomato purée

1 small pumpkin or winter squash, diced

(makes about 4 cups)

2 medium potatoes, diced

1 can chickpeas (garbanzo beans), drained

1½ teaspoon curry powder

½ teaspoon turmeric

½ teaspoon garam masala spice blend

½ teaspoon ground clove

1   In a large soup pot, sauté onion and carrot purée/mince in butter and oil for 3-4 minutes.

2   Add water and tomato dice/purée and bring to a boil. Add pumpkin, potatoes, chickpeas, and spices. Boil until pumpkin and potatoes are easily pierced with a fork. Serve alone or over cooked rice.

Fresh Persimmon Curry

SERVES 4–6

I like to make curries in the fall not only because they are so easy to make and taste so good, but also because I can put in lots of the spice turmeric, which is anti-inflammatory and helps the body stave off colds and flu. If you are not familiar with this spice, here is some information on turmeric from the U.S. National Library of Medicine:

> *"Turmeric is a plant. You probably know turmeric as the main spice in curry. It has a warm, bitter taste and is frequently used to flavor or color curry powders, mustards, butters, and cheeses. But the root of turmeric is also used widely to make medicine. Turmeric is used for arthritis, heartburn (dyspepsia), stomach pain, diarrhea, intestinal gas, stomach bloating, loss of appetite, jaundice, liver problems, and gallbladder disorders. It is also used for headaches, bronchitis, colds, lung infections, fibromyalgia, leprosy, fever, menstrual problems, and cancer. Other uses include depression, Alzheimer's disease, water retention, worms, and kidney problems. Some people apply turmeric to the skin for pain, ringworm, bruising, leech bites, eye infections, inflammatory skin conditions, soreness inside of the mouth, and infected wounds."*

SOURCE:http://www.nlm.nih.gov/medlineplus/druginfo/natural/662.html

The onions in this curry recipe are also anti-inflammatory and great for people with sinus issues.

Persimmons are one of my favorite fruits of all time. When I lived in Japan, I would walk down the streets and there would be trees loaded with persimmons, just like apple trees in America. I had never seen nor eaten a persimmon before I lived in Japan, but I immediately loved them and I was known to eat a half-dozen in one sitting. Persimmons sort of look like flat tomatoes, but they taste like a cross between an apricot, a pear, and an apple. They are wonderful. Persimmon curry is a very Japanese recipe–the Japanese love to eat curry and rice. In the U.S., persimmons come into season in late fall. They are great when eaten raw like an apple (the persimmon skin is tough, so you'll want to peel it), and they are great in curry. So without further ado, here is my recipe:

1½ cups of rice, to be cooked

3 medium onions, diced

3 carrots, sliced

1 tablespoon olive oil

1 tablespoon flour

1 tablespoon olive oil (again)

1 cup milk (or coconut milk)

½ teaspoon curry powder (for mild curry. Double if you like spicy curry)

1 tablespoon turmeric

2 fresh persimmons, diced

1 breaded chicken breast filet per person (I just buy this at my local supermarket deli to make life easier. Breaded pork chops are also excellent.)

1 Put the rice on to cook. I use a $10 rice cooker from Walmart that we've had for many years. In Japan, a rice cooker is a household necessity!

2 In a heavy-bottomed skillet or enameled cast iron pan, begin to sauté the onions in the first tablespoon of oil over medium heat. Add the carrots, cover the pan, and lower the heat to low. Cook for 8–10 minutes, until carrots are soft.

3 In your pan, push the onions and carrots to the edges of the pan to clear a space in the center. In this center hole, add the second tablespoon of oil and the flour. Stir the oil and flour together and cook over medium heat for one minute, and then stir in the vegetables. Add the milk, curry, and turmeric and bring to a simmer for 3–4 minutes.

4 Turn off the heat. Add the diced fresh persimmon. Serve over rice. Slice the breaded chicken breasts and serve on top of the curry. Enjoy!

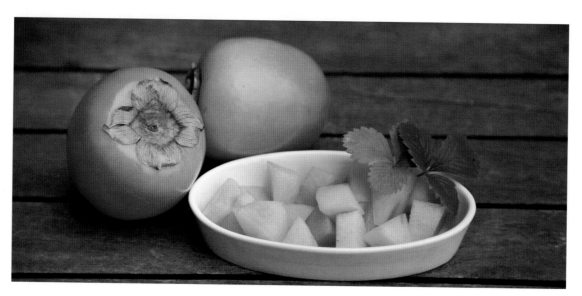

Pizza

I confess that I have an addiction to my own homemade pizza. I'm proud to say I can make two large, four-topping pizzas in 15 minutes–including scratch dough and sauce! You can too. (15 minutes does not include dough raising or baking time.) Beware! You will probably become addicted to this too! I make this pizza once a week. I dream about this pizza, and crave it. This week, as I write this, I made it all the way to Tuesday before making pizza!

Pizza Dough

We only use natural yeast pizza dough. If you are not familiar with the health and nutrition benefits of natural yeast, you'll find answers is my co-authored book, The Art of Baking With Natural Yeast. Because using natural yeast is nothing like using store-bought yeast, it wouldn't help to repeat here the recipe for pizza dough found in that book. If you don't want to make your own scratch dough, most bakeries and grocery store bakeries sell fresh, ready-to-use dough.

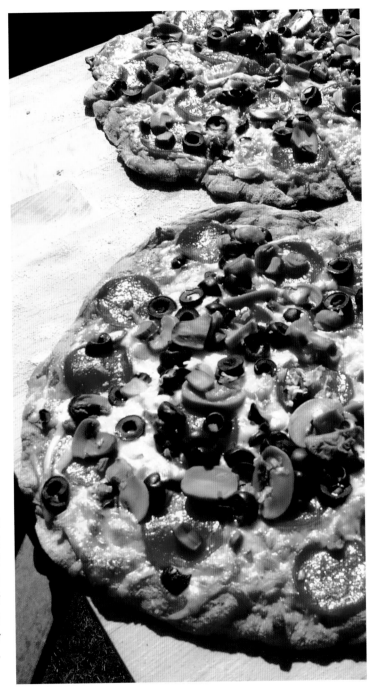

Traditional Tomato Pizza Sauce

Two large tomatoes, or four medium, or eight small

½ teaspoon dried basil

¼ teaspoon dried oregano

¼ teaspoon dried marjoram

¼ teaspoon dried thyme

¼ teaspoon dried parsley

Two carrots, grated, OR grated beet (optional)

½ teaspoon salt

1 Combine all ingredients in a blender or food processor until smooth.

2 Cook over medium heat in a sauce pan for 20–30 minutes.

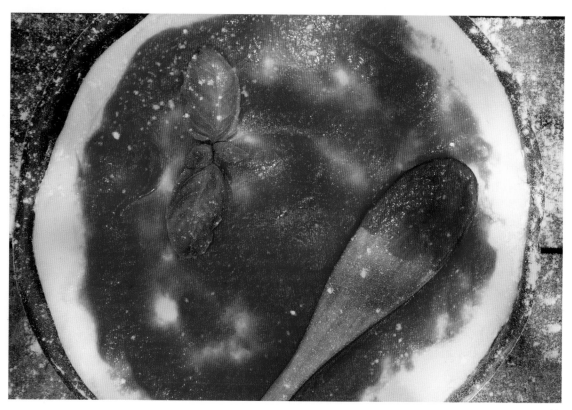

Fresh Instant Tomato Pizza Sauce

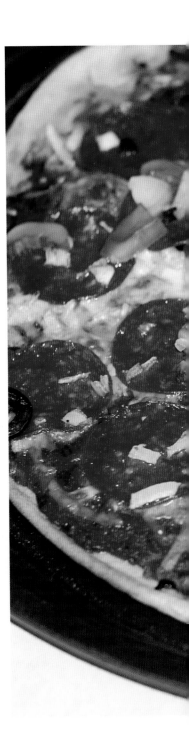

I discovered the key to the world's fastest, fresh, homemade pizza sauce completely by accident–which is how most great recipes are discovered! My friend, Melissa Richardson, and I wrote a cookbook called The Art of Baking With Natural Yeast, *published in 2012. One day, before the book came out, we were co-teaching a natural yeast baking class in a classroom kitchen. One of the recipes we demonstrated was pizza. But when it came time to put the toppings on the crust, we realized we had completely forgotten to make the scratch sauce. Thinking fast, we put the tomatoes in a blender whole, putting the raw puréed tomatoes on as the sauce.*

Lo and behold, it was delicious. So light and fresh tasting. I've made my pizza sauce this way ever since. Here's how:

Two large tomatoes, or four medium, or eight small

½ teaspoon salt

1   Rinse whole tomatoes, from the garden if you have them. You can also use home-bottled tomatoes (minus the liquid), or whole frozen tomatoes. Purée them in the blender. (If you are using whole, frozen tomatoes, start with ⅛ cup hot water and one frozen tomato in the blender, adding one tomato at a time.)

2   Add salt. Spread the purée on crusts. Be sure to spread all the way to the edges of the pizza.

3   Sprinkle each crust with 1 teaspoon of homemade pizza seasoning, using the herbs listed in the Traditional Tomato Pizza Sauce recipe above.

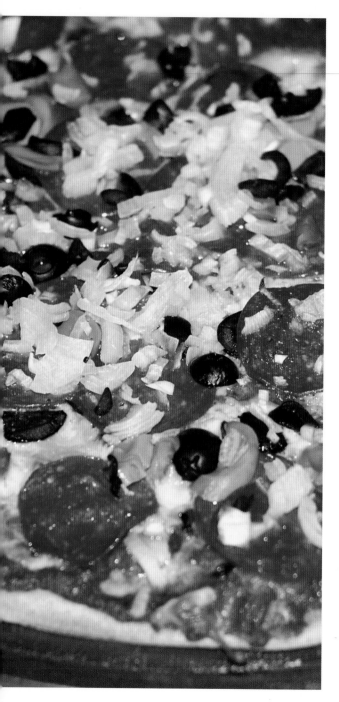

Pizza Toppings

There are three kinds of pizza—the kind I like, and the kind my wife, Charmayne, wants, and the pizza kids love.

Caleb's pizza toppings

Sliced black olives, sliced mushrooms, pepperoni, and sweet Italian sausage

Pizza for kids

Cheese, olives, and julienne carrots: that's what they like at our house! I usually make a half-pizza for them. They love to put toppings on pizza. Let them spread the cheese and decorate with pepperonis and scatter the mushrooms. Make sure they get to choose what they want on their half!

Charmayne's pizza

My wife prefers true Italian pizza, which is healthier, lighter (as in less greasy), and fresher than traditional American pizza.

White Alfredo pizza sauce, feta or parmesan cheese, or slices of mozzarella, chicken (optional), sliced fresh tomatoes (or sun-dried), and whole, fresh spinach or basil leaves.

Alfredo Pizza Sauce

2 tablespoons butter

2 tablespoons whole-wheat flour

pinch of salt

1 cup milk OR half-and-half OR ½ cup cream and ½ cup vegetable or chicken broth

½ cup grated cheese

1 Melt the butter in a pan over medium heat. Stir in the flour. Cook while stirring for one minute. (This is called a roux in French cuisine [pronounced roo]. This recipe is a traditional roux sauce.)

2 Add salt and milk. Add cheese of your choice. If you use block cheese like cheddar (instead of a dry cheese like Parmesan, romano, or mitzithra), add an extra tablespoon of flour. Whisk over medium heat until smooth and begins to thicken. Let cool for a couple of minutes to thicken more before spreading over pizza crust.

True Italian Pizza

Genuine Italian pizza is always made with fresh yeast, coincidentally! Italian toppings are nothing like the pizza found in America. These are lighter, fresher pizzas than pizza in this country. Here are some suggestions:

Quattro Formaggi

(Traditional Four Cheese Pizza–popular all over Italy) Brush the crust with olive oil. Scatter a combination of romano, feta, Parmesan, and ricotta. Enjoy!

Margherita

(Tomato Mozzarella) Cover crust in Alfredo white sauce. Cover with strips (not grated) of mozzarella cheese. Top with slices of fresh tomatoes and fresh basil leaves.

Basil Cheese

Brush the crust with olive oil infused with fresh roasted garlic. Put fresh oregano and basil leaves under and over a combination of romano, feta, Parmesan, and ricotta. Enjoy!